Charles Rose, Architect

Charles Rose, Architect

Graham Foundation for Advanced Studies in the Fine Arts, Chicago
Princeton Architectural Press, New York

Graham Foundation/Princeton Architectural Press
New Voices in Architecture
presents first monographs on emerging designers
from around the world

Also available in this series:

Rick Joy: Desert Works
1-56898-336-0

ARO: Architecture Research Office
1-56898-367-0

Julie Snow Architects
1-56898-487-1

An Architecture of the Ozarks:
The Works of Marlon Blackwell
1-56898-488-X

Plain Modern:
The Architecture of Brian MacKay-Lyons
1-56898-477-4

Published by
Princeton Architectural Press
37 East Seventh Street
New York, New York 10003

For a free catalog of books, call 1.800.722.6657.
Visit our web site at www.papress.com.

Editing: Linda Lee
Design: Jan Haux

Special thanks to: Nettie Aljian, Dorothy Ball,
Nicola Bednarek, Janet Behning, Megan Carey,
Becca Casbon, Penny (Yuen Pik) Chu, Russell
Fernandez, Clare Jacobson, John King, Mark
Lamster, Nancy Eklund Later, Katharine Myers,
Lauren Nelson, Scott Tennent, Jennifer Thompson,
Paul Wagner, Joseph Weston, Tiffany Wey,
and Deb Wood of Princeton Architectural Press
—Kevin C. Lippert, publisher

All drawings, rendering, and model photographs
© Charles Rose Architects, Inc.
All photographs © Charles Rose Architects, Inc.
unless otherwise noted.

Chuck Choi
2, 30, 33–35, 37–41, 44–46, 48–49, 98,100 top,
101 top, 103–25, 136, 139–49, 176, 179–83,
185–87, 192–93, 197, 199, 201–2, 206 bottom
row, 207, 212–17
John Linden
8, 11–13, 15–17, 19–29, 42–43, 47, 50, 53–57,
59–60, 64–65, 66 top, 68–69, 70, 73–75, 76 top,
77 top, 78–89, 160, 163–65, 167–75
Greg Premru
61–63, 66 bottom, 67
Steve Rosenthal
206 top
Willard Traub
203 bottom row

Library of Congress Cataloging-in-Publication Data
Rose, Charles, 1960–
  Charles Rose, architect.
    p. cm. — (New voices in architecture)
  Includes bibliographical references.
  ISBN 1-56898-537-1 (pbk. : alk. paper)
  1. Rose, Charles, 1960- 2. Architecture—United
States—21st century. 3. Architecture—United
States—20th century. I. Title. II. Series.
  NA737.R65A4 2006
  720'.92—dc22
                                    2005020585

Table of Contents

Foreword

Terence Riley

In Henry James's novel *The Europeans*, the protagonist's relatives come to visit America and comment on the openness of the New England countryside, referring to it as an "uncastled" landscape. Charles Rose's architecture seems to have sprung from a similar sentiment. Rather than dominate the site and its surroundings, his architecture habitually seeks the contours rather than the crest. Whether the topography is dramatic or subtle, Rose's instinct is to reinforce the geometries of the site, at times making the viewers more aware of the landscape than they might have been otherwise.

Rather than idealizing architectural form, Rose privileges the landscape's tendency to singular expression. Above the structures, the roof planes invariably hover, seeking not the level of the horizon but the exceptional forms of the landscape without as well as the flow of activities within. Moreover, his structures generally meet the ground in a subtle way, feathered into the landscape by walkways and terraces, rejecting the formal podium that so often defined the relationship between classical architecture—as well as classic modernism—and nature. While his architecture most certainly has urban implications, Rose's work to date is most convincing in its ability to make an Arcadian vision legible.

Rose's attitude toward the modern past is expanded by a sense of freedom with geometry. While Breuer and Le Corbusier cautiously departed from their strict sense of geometric form in the "butterfly" roofs of the exhibition house in the garden of MoMA and the Erasuriz houses in Chile, respectively, Rose's manipulation of form more fully embraces a catalogue of prismatic strategies. Even so, this expansive attitude is never detached from the logic of construction. Digital design has opened up a whole new vocabulary of geometric possibilities, yet Rose's work is not defined by geometric complexity *per se*, but tethered to the norms of the construction industry prevalent today. While we may live in a world that is only knowable through the physics of relativity, our day-to-day experience—particularly how we make things—is more familiar. As Italo Calvino noted, "the heavy machines still exist," if they are now controlled by weightless bits. In Rose's architecture, the philosophical impurity of Calvino's observation is made a virtue.

Orleans House

Cape Cod, Massachusetts, 2004

This project expresses much of the approach to design that I have developed over the last two decades. I view design as a process of investigation, and I resist committing to a concept until it has gone through many iterations. I tend to make forms that are sculptural, active, and somewhat enigmatic. They're not driven by type or history. They are knit into the landscape, rather than objects imposed on it. It is my hope that people will read this house not as an object, but as an experience of movement through the building and site.

Orleans House, which sits on a bluff overlooking Pleasant Bay, was an ideal project: the clients, Alison and John Ferring of St. Louis, were game to approach architecture as a process of exploration. This was not without risk: we faced a real obstacle in overcoming local assumptions that Cape houses must be historical in character. Nonetheless, we came up with six schemes and built models of them all. Each took a different approach to site, circulation, and the clients' wish for a year-round main house with an art studio/guest quarters and office.

The design we developed is an extension of the landform. Low slung and one room deep at all points, the main house traces a natural bowl and is intricately woven into the landscape. No regrading was done; no mature trees were removed. All these features, I believe, helped us win approval from the local historical commission.

The Orleans House plans express a lot of free movement. I may bend a wall to create a better fit to the site, to improve circulation, or to create more of a sculptural effect as I investigate interior space and exterior form making. Structurally, the house is a hybrid: a wood-frame structure with load-bearing walls is combined with a steel frame with slender stainless-steel columns. Seaside, this allowed us to open the house to light and water using large planes of glass. On the exterior, different materials are juxtaposed to enhance form and create scale. Large roof planes, made of lead-coated copper panels, alternately create large open spaces and small, protected spaces, for example. In addition, low exterior walls are made of highly crafted cast-in-place board-formed concrete, which leaves the imprint of wood; elsewhere, cedar siding and wood panels create humanly scaled episodes.

1   Spa
2   Terrace
3   Dining terrace
4   Screen porch
5   Dining room
6   Kitchen
7   Living room
8   Foyer
9   Library/Media room
10 Master bedroom
11 Bedroom
12 Motor court
13 Family/Bunk room
14 Guest house

Site plan

Roof plan

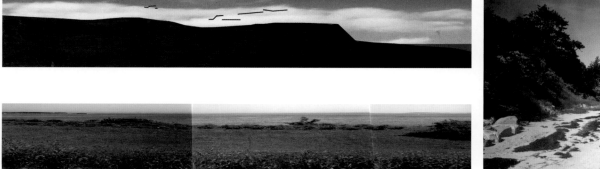

Site section looking east

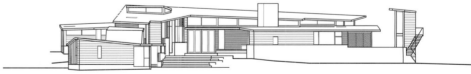

North elevation

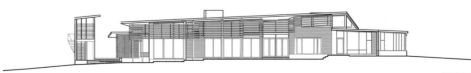

South elevation

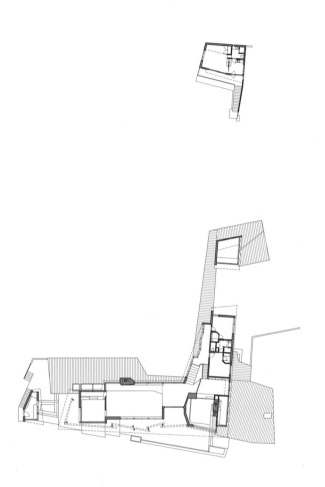

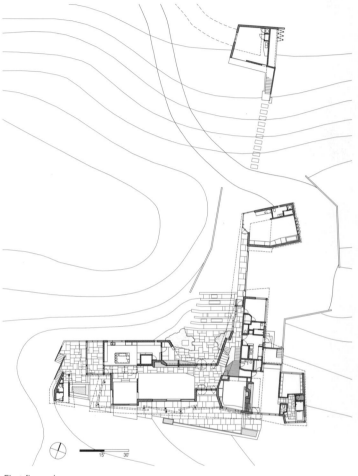

Second floor plan

First floor plan

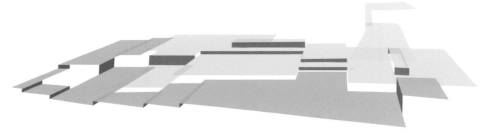

Levels of occupation

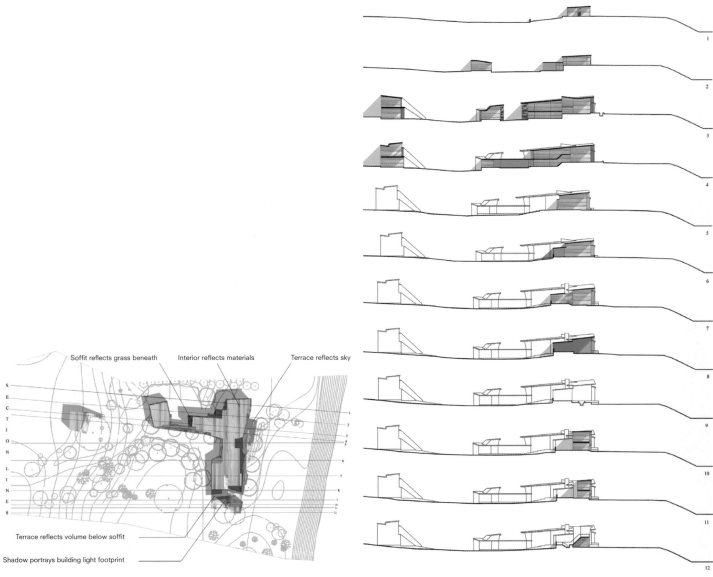

Soffit reflects grass beneath   Interior reflects materials   Terrace reflects sky

S
E
C
T
I
O
N

L
I
N
E
S

Terrace reflects volume below soffit

Shadow portrays building light footprint

Material studies plan

Material studies sections

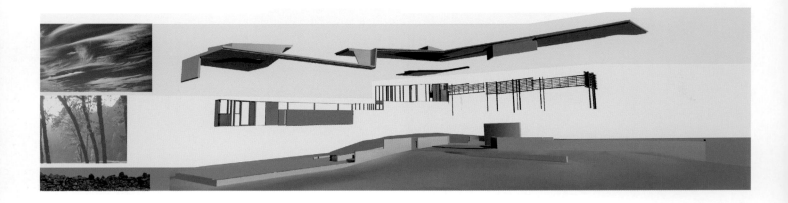

Carl and Ruth Shapiro Campus Center, Brandeis University

Waltham, Massachusetts, 2002

Brandeis, founded in 1948, is a modernist campus with a naturalistic landscape. The campus boasts a number of notable, modernist pavilions that appear as orthogonal objects in the landscape. We sought to design a building that would stand, in contrast, as a part of the topography and define landscapes through its forms and mass.

We chose for the site a parking lot and aging building, which sat at the geographical heart of the campus. These were demolished. The location of the center made the symbolic gesture of placing students at the core of the university, where two major pedestrian axes crossed. This site plan created significant new landscapes, including a courtyard, gardens, and an expansive central green space, which the postwar campus lacked. The new green space links the center with the admissions and administrative buildings, an art museum, and a large theater.

The center, two buildings connected by a three-story atrium, is a set of blunt sculptural forms. Massing echoes the rock outcroppings found around the region and connotes these simple muscular landscape forms. Fossilized limestone cladding adds warmth to the abstract forms and recalls its traditional use in honorific buildings on the campus. The entire exterior of the north side is clad in pre-patinaed copper panels, chosen because they enhance the building's sculptural volume. The circulation plan makes student activity highly visible. The atrium is crisscrossed by bridges that connect the center's upper levels. Abundant glass allows views that constantly reconnect visitors to the surrounding campus.

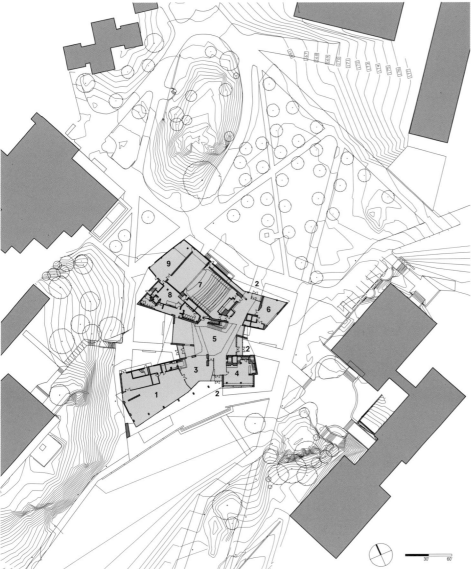

1 Bookstore
2 Entry
3 Cafe
4 Library
5 Atrium
6 Lounge
7 Auditorium
8 Green room
9 Backstage

Site plan

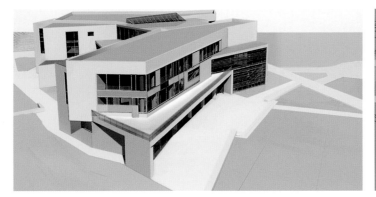
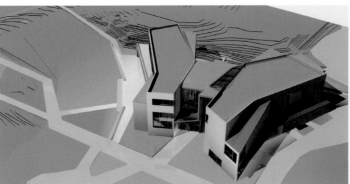

South elevation

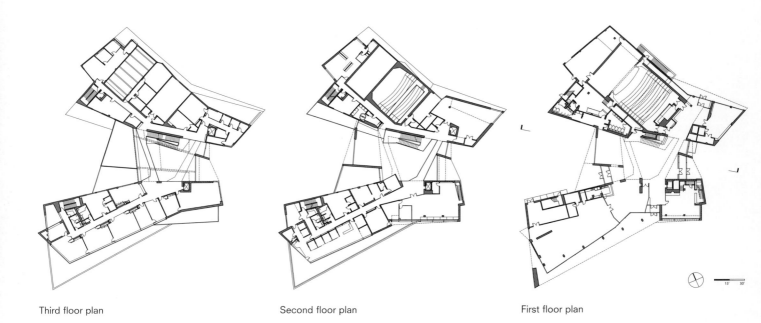

Third floor plan

Second floor plan

First floor plan

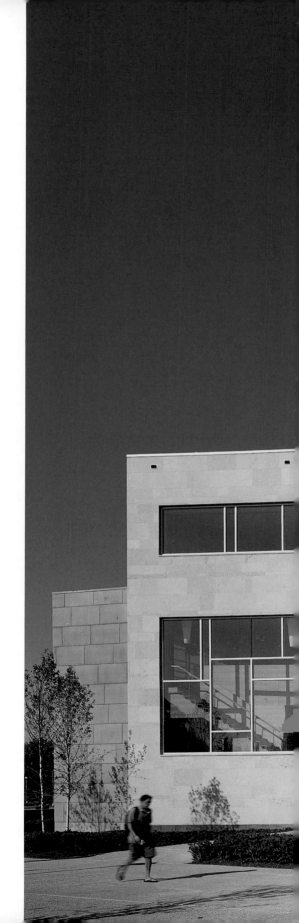

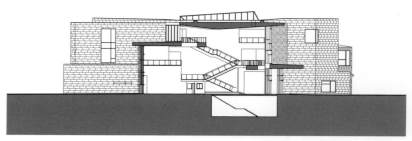

Section looking north

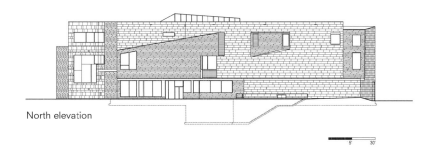

North elevation

Currier Center for the Performing Arts, The Putney School

Putney, Vermont, 2004

The performing arts center offered the challenge of introducing contemporary architecture into a rural hilltop campus. Putney, a boarding school and working farm, was a collection of historic clapboard buildings and a red barn when we started working on this project with students, faculty, and trustees. The center's program—an auditorium, dance studio, and rehearsal and exhibition space—called for a building far larger than any other structure on the intimately scaled campus. We were acutely sensitive to minimizing the building's potential impact as an ungainly intruder. The site we chose preserves the campus-defining open spaces to the east and west, and sits next to a white clapboard building snug against a hill.

As the design developed, we broke down the mass of the building. The roof—folded and fragmented—reflects this impulse and our desire to make an organic structure. Building forms are embedded topographically into the site, and the aggregate massing alludes to the historic massing of New England farmhouses and successfully reduces the scalar impact of the building.

Inside, gallery spaces serve as an interior promenade linked to the campus path system; views along this path continuously reconnect visitors to the landscape. Fissures in the folded roof plane create slots that bring light into the colored studios. The roof by the hill is planted with sedums, which makes a literal connection to the ground but, more importantly, helped qualify the center to receive a Leadership in Energy and Environmental Design (LEED) certification from the U.S. Green Building Council.

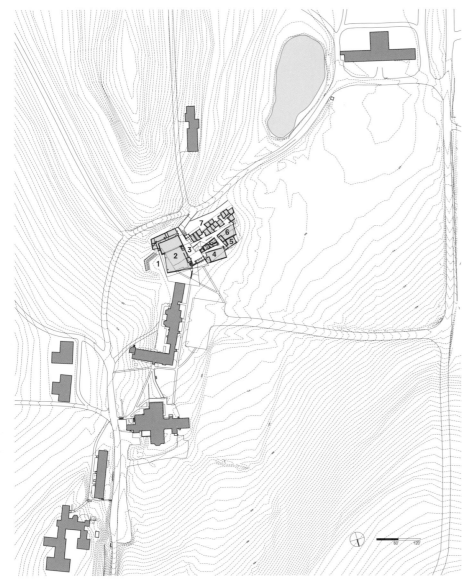

1 Amphitheater
2 Auditorium
3 Gallery
4 Dance studio
5 Seminar room
6 Orchestral/Choral room
7 Practice rooms and offices

Site plan

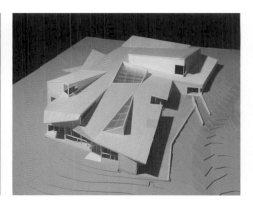

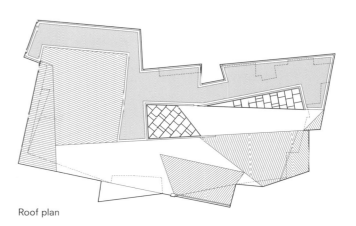

Roof plan

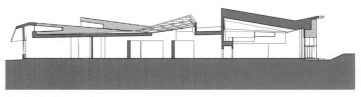

Section looking east

Section looking north

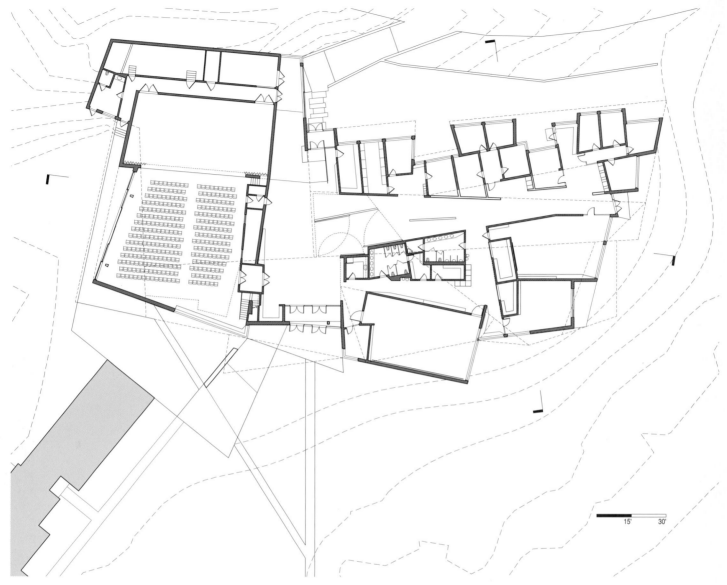

Floor plan

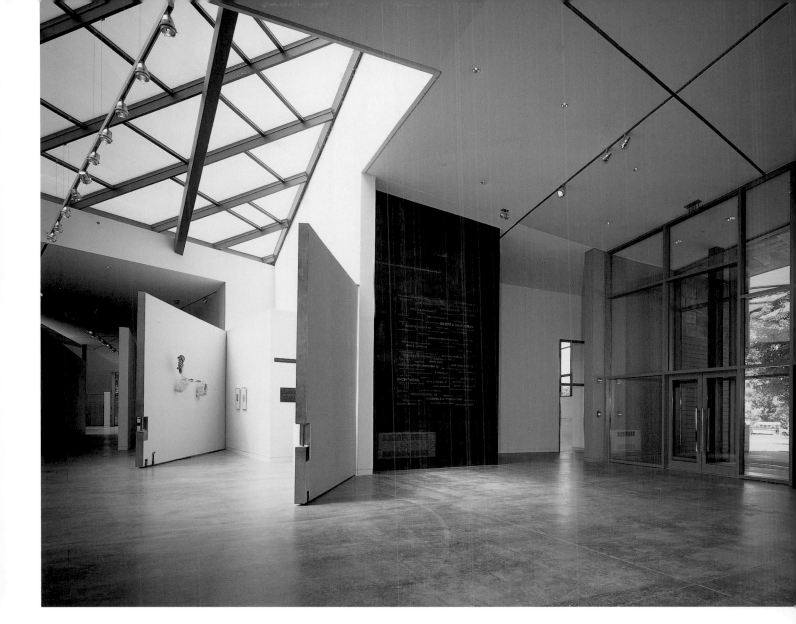

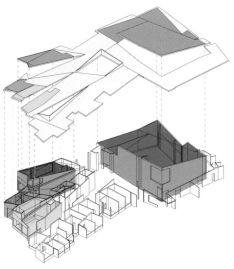

Volumes and roof planes

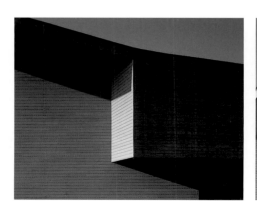

Copper House

Massachusetts, 2004

I typically resist renovations, but this project was compelling—it was my house. The architecture itself did not warrant saving. A vinyl-clad Colonial knockoff, it was poorly sited, and a garage separated the house from a gracious yard. Although its small, low-ceilinged rooms did not give my wife and me the living and work space we needed, it did possess a number of cozy areas, and some young but persuasive voices lobbied for its preservation.

The design marries a two-story copper and glass addition to the existing three-story Colonial. We demolished the garage, which allowed us to connect new living spaces to the yard. The most difficult problem was integrating the existing house with the new building. The scale was inconsistent: ceilings and floors did not align, and the volumes of boxlike rooms in the Colonial contrasted starkly with the open, light-filled spaces of the addition. Traditional windows in the Colonial seemed quaint at best compared to the walls of glass planned for the addition.

We solved the most glaring problem of fit by putting the Colonial in a new wrapper—a cedar box. We left the Colonial's windows as they were (although we replaced the old faux panes with new frames and single sheets of glass), which on the exterior creates a punched-in quality on an otherwise severe facade. Nor did we want to entirely hide the original house: the cedar boards are slightly separated so that light seeps through and the old forms can be glimpsed. To confront the central problem—how to stitch together the old and new inside—we exposed this potential conflict in the most public place: the entryway. One walks through the front door into the divide, which is a three-story atrium, with the old house on the right and addition on the left. The sense of a divide is further heightened—and resolved—by a sculptural steel-and-glass stair bridge, visible upon entry. The ground-floor stairs, dining room server and fireplace are designed as sculptural pieces that have their own function but also delineate room areas.

20' 40'

1 Carport
2 Storage
3 Guestroom
4 Library
5 Music room
6 Project room
7 Patio
8 Living room
9 Dining room
10 Kitchen
11 Terrace
12 Entry

Demolition and site plan

Demolition/Original Garage
Existing to Remain
New Construction

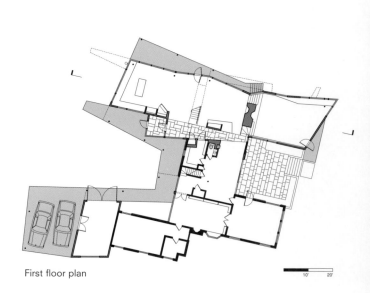

Second floor plan

First floor plan

10' 20'

Material and volume study

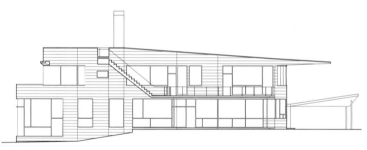

North elevation

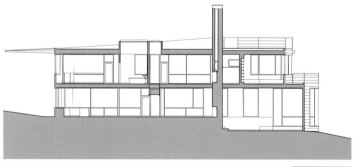

Section looking north

10' 20'

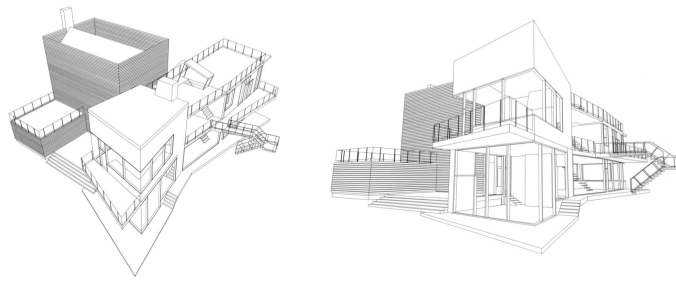

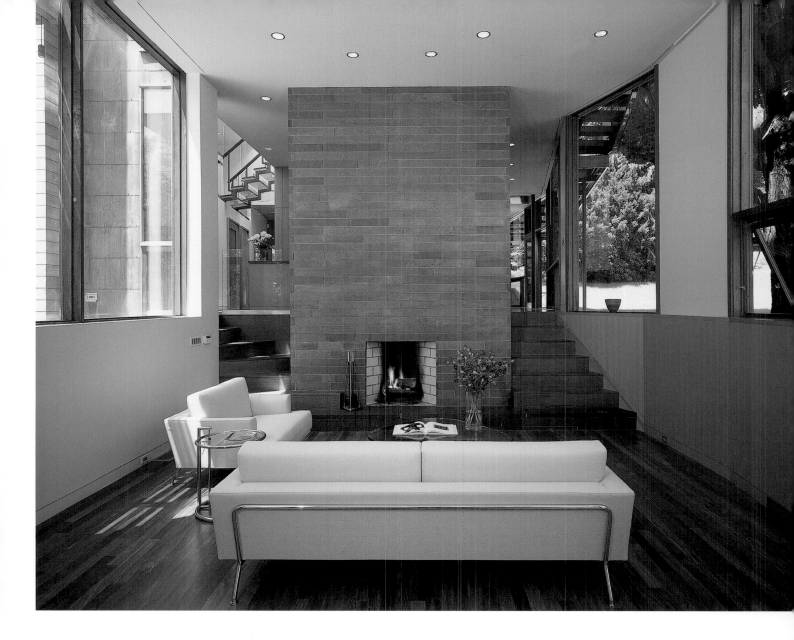

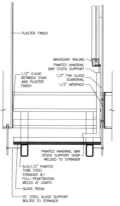

Handrail and stair detail

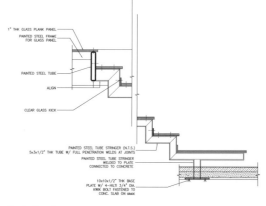

Stair detail

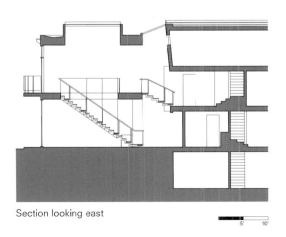

Section looking east

5'   10'

United States Port of Entry

Del Rio, Texas, 2004

This U.S.-Mexico border crossing station is the first of several commissions we have received from the U.S. General Services Administration's Design Excellence program. This program selects leading American architects for federal buildings, such as Richard Meier's acclaimed federal courthouse in Islip, Long Island.

The project needed a powerful architectural symbol that was imbued with openness and optimism. Yet as we investigated the building type, we found a number of competing needs that added complexity to the design process. Although we wanted the station to feel open and welcoming, the nature of the work there required that it be completely controlled and secure. Ample daylight was essential to security functions, yet screening out the searing Texas sun was just as important for employees' comfort.

The primary canopy—a soaring steel structure 370 feet wide and 85 feet deep, covering the northbound commercial and noncommercial lanes—can be seen from a great distance, hovering above the surrounding Rio Grande flood plain. The secondary canopy, under which passenger vehicle inspection takes place, is 200 feet wide and 350 feet deep. In the design of the secondary canopy, we sought to resolve the inherent tensions between the needs for security and openness, and light and shade. We drew on some of our previous work in Florida, particularly the Gulf Coast Museum of Art, where we used light monitors to filter the harsh sun and bring in ambient northern light to the galleries. Similarly, we designed large north-facing slots in the secondary steel canopy at Del Rio, using computer-aided lighting software to adjust their size until we were certain that they supplied ample ambient light below. Shades of white and light gray were painted on the canopy's underside to reflect light to the lanes below. The slots also function as natural vents oriented toward prevailing winds so that they draw fumes from idling cars and trucks away from the inspection area.

The design addresses many issues, from efficient vehicular inspection to a harsh microclimate. Secure gardens provide respite for employees, and small pedestrian connectors provide shaded cover for employees and visitors as they move about the site. Large subterranean ducts further disperse fumes by mechanically redistributing air. Gardens and landscapes were designed as "sustainable" and feature drought-tolerant plants, grids of shade trees, and fountains for evaporative cooling.

East elevation

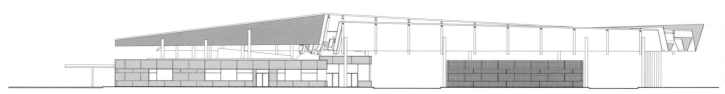

North elevation

West elevation

20'   40'

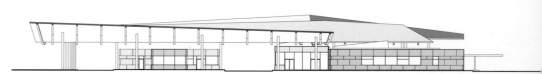

Section looking north

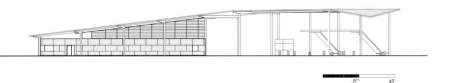

2'   40'

1 Entry into the United States
2 Exit into Mexico
3 Primary inspection building
4 Secondary inspection area
5 Administration building
6 Kennel building
7 Empty truck inspection
8 Existing commercial inspection area

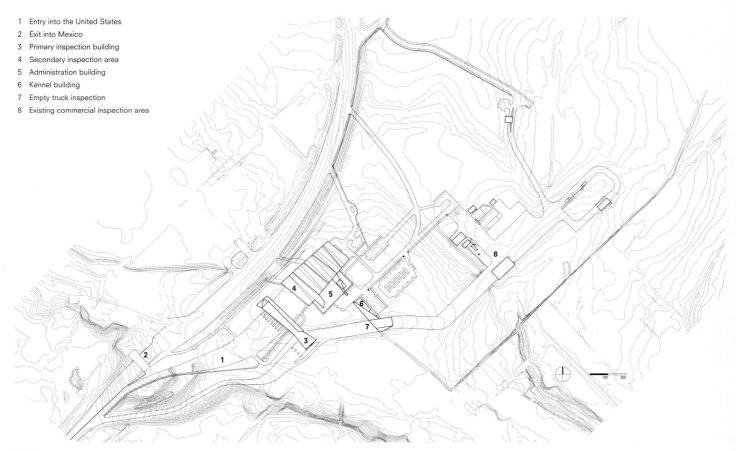

Site plan

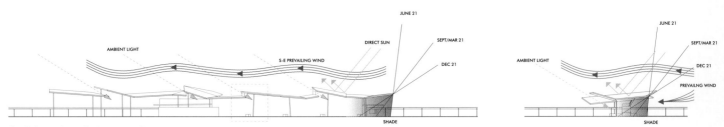

Daylight and ventilation strategies

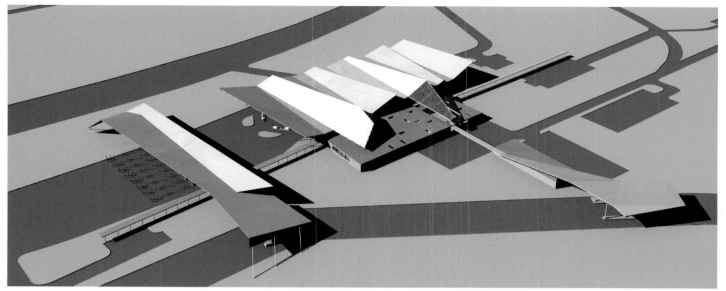

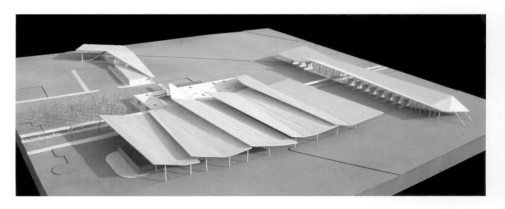

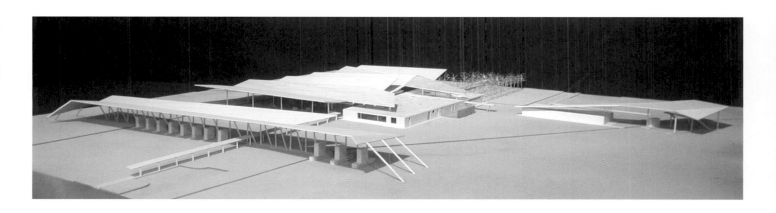

Camp Paint Rock

Hyattville, Wyoming, 2000

The Alm Foundation, a private Los Angeles–based charity, commissioned us to build a camp for underprivileged teenagers on rugged ranchland in north-central Wyoming. Set amid tall mesas and steep canyon land, Paint Rock is a summer camp serving a foundation program for inner-city Los Angeles teens that also offers academic support and guidance. The complex consists of sixteen buildings, including boys' and girls' cabins, a dining hall, director's house, counselors' lodge, and a stable, clustered around the mouth of a canyon.

Paint Rock's design seeks to capture the dramatic scale, power, and beauty of the West. Building forms echo the geology and natural shapes of the landscape. The roof of the dining hall, for example, is inspired by geologic fault lines: fissures create openings for views up the canyon and allow in natural light. Many of the cabins were built on steel platforms and stilts that burrow into the canyon walls. Decks, lookouts, and sliding barnlike doors open these light, primitive buildings to the skies and sweeping views. The buildings, with their metal roofs, appear as glinting shards in the bright western sun. Together, they form a kind of neatly fractured community. Each building stands independently but connects through a series of pathways and bridges, which in turn reinforces through design the camp philosophy of self-reliance and leadership within an interdependent community.

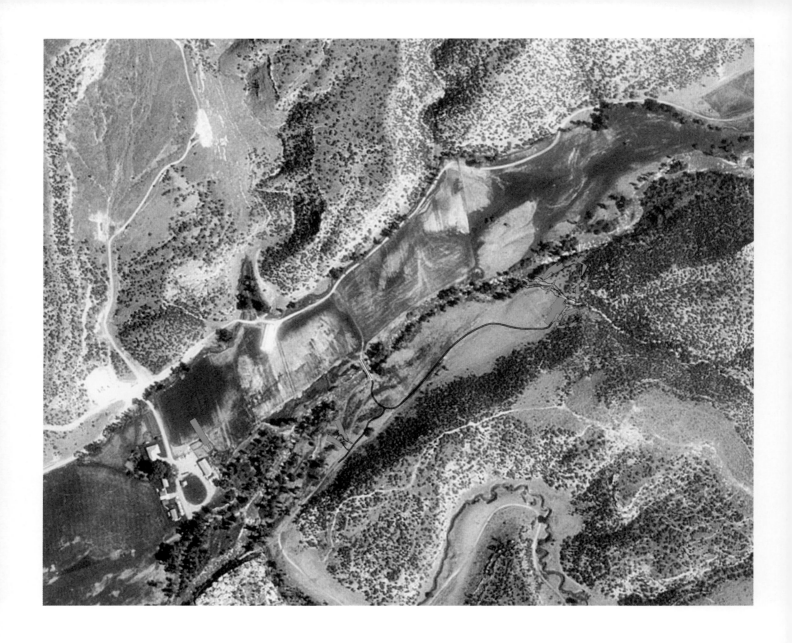

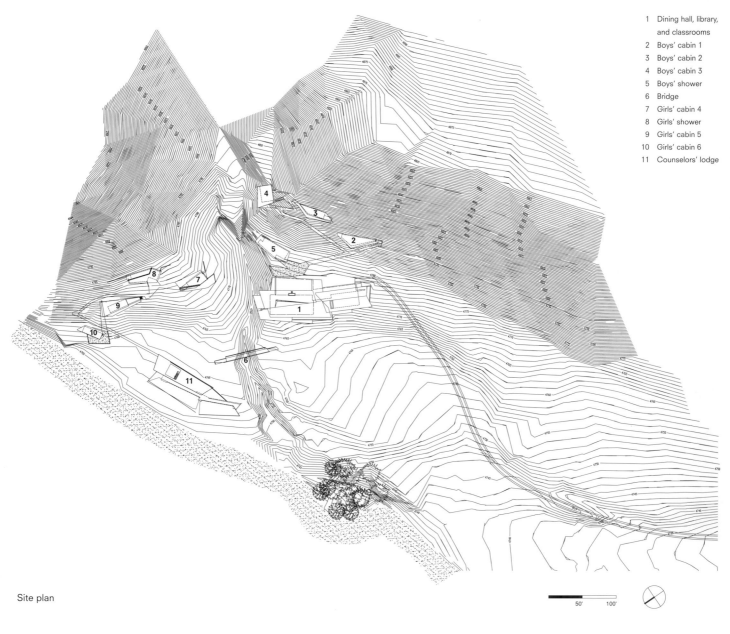

1   Dining hall, library,
    and classrooms
2   Boys' cabin 1
3   Boys' cabin 2
4   Boys' cabin 3
5   Boys' shower
6   Bridge
7   Girls' cabin 4
8   Girls' shower
9   Girls' cabin 5
10 Girls' cabin 6
11 Counselors' lodge

Site plan

50'   100'

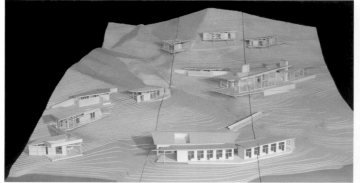

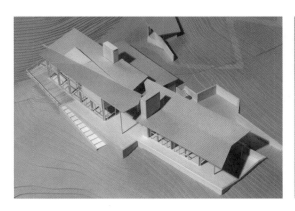

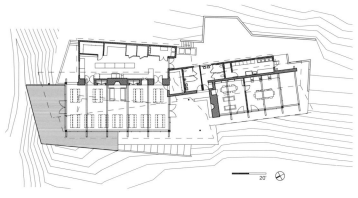

Dining hall plan

Dining hall west elevation

Dinging hall south elevation

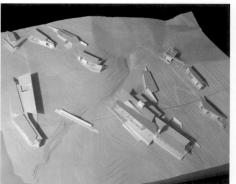

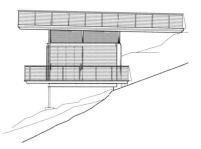

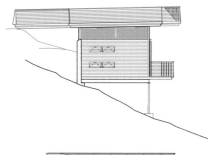

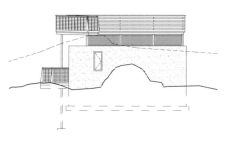

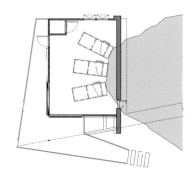

Cabin 3: section, elevations, plan

111

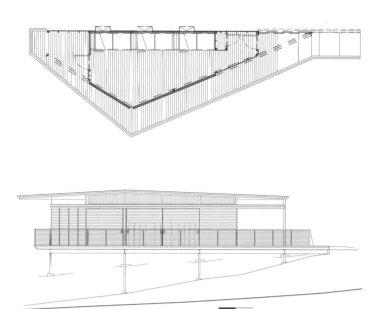

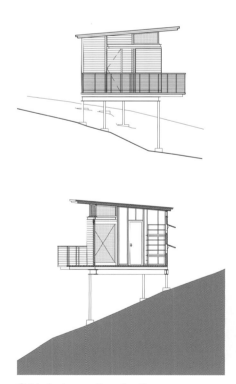

Cabin 1: plan, section, elevations

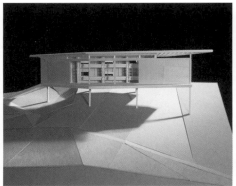

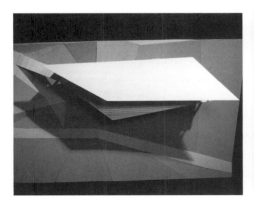
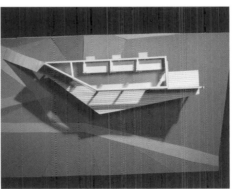

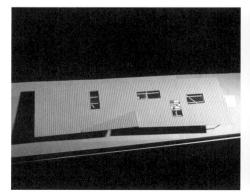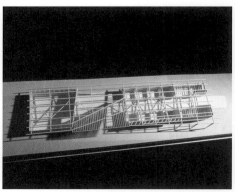

Booker T. Washington High School for the Performing and Visual Arts, Competition

Dallas, Texas, 2001

There was a vibrant confluence in this project of the site and the school's mission. Seated at the edge of the downtown Dallas Arts District, the new school is part of a cluster of distinguished arts buildings—opera, theater, museums, and an outdoor sculpture garden.

Our design, selected as one of four finalists for a competition sponsored by the National Endowment for the Arts, sought to support the school's educational goals and connect students and faculty directly to the visual and performing arts surrounding them. The plan substantially added to an existing historic brick building, which had to be preserved, and also responded to the site's gritty urban character. In our design, we pushed the mass of the building to the site's northern, eastern, and southern perimeters. Expressed as blunt sculptural forms, the masses confront the freeway, city streets, and rubble lots just beyond and, notably, create a southwest-facing courtyard that opens to the Arts District and Dallas skyline.

The main entrance is on the southwest corner, through the courtyard. As one enters, the angled forms of the roofscape emerge, with some roof planes merging with the courtyard. Our design was formally influenced by I. M. Pei and Partners' nearby Fountain Place tower; it transforms the tower's elegant vertical sculpturalism into an angled horizontal composition. Our intention with the sloped roofs was to introduce an intriguing topographical element that contrasted with the overall flatness of the area. Additionally, these constructed planes resonate with the sometimes-dramatic freeway overpasses and offer a series of new vantage points from which to view the city, the Arts District, and the school. The roofs were to be planted with sod, a "sustainable" feature that positively affected the site's microclimate by reducing heat gain in the summer.

For the school's interior, we intended to foster opportunities for informal conversations and fortuitous encounters that encourage cross-fertilization between the disciplines. Corridor space is minimized. Circulation spaces also serve as galleries. Common spaces and separate galleries flow into areas of circulation and reinforce an atmosphere of openness and interaction.

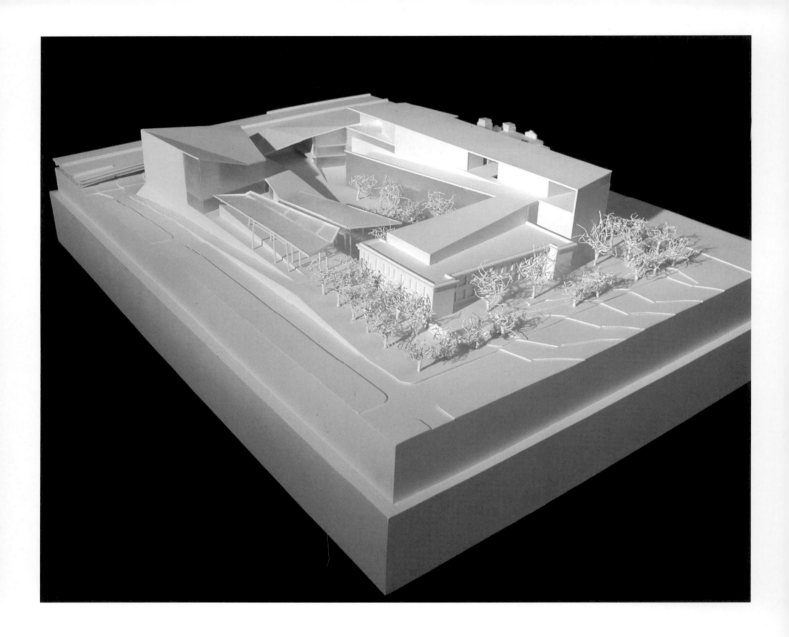

Site program and massing

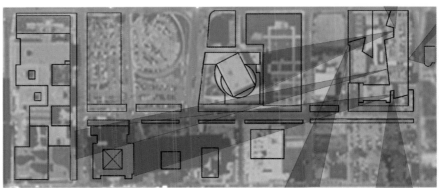

Views of downtown from site

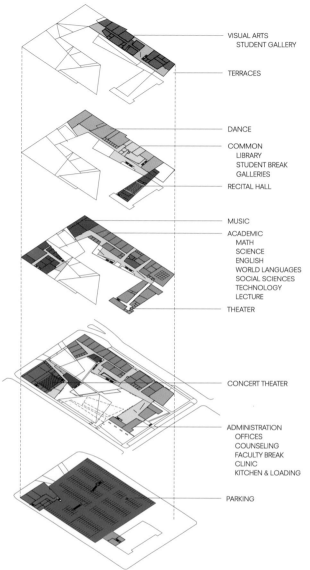

VISUAL ARTS
  STUDENT GALLERY

TERRACES

DANCE

COMMON
  LIBRARY
  STUDENT BREAK
  GALLERIES

RECITAL HALL

MUSIC
ACADEMIC
  MATH
  SCIENCE
  ENGLISH
  WORLD LANGUAGES
  SOCIAL SCIENCES
  TECHNOLOGY
  LECTURE

THEATER

CONCERT THEATER

ADMINISTRATION
  OFFICES
  COUNSELING
  FACULTY BREAK
  CLINIC
  KITCHEN & LOADING

PARKING

Programmatic diagram

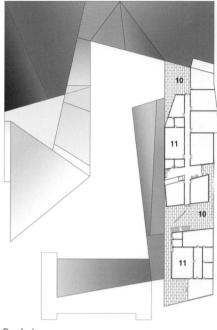

Roof plan

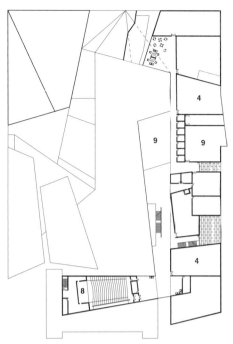

Third floor plan

1 Concert theater
2 Outdoor theater
3 Academic spaces
4 Dance
5 Administration
6 Music
7 Theater
8 Recital hall
9 Common areas (library, student break, galleries)
10 Terraces
11 Visual arts

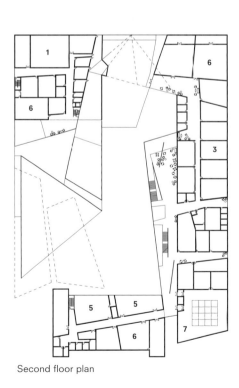

Second floor plan

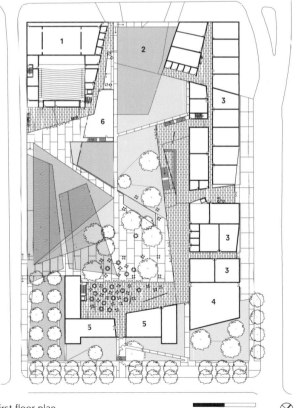

First floor plan

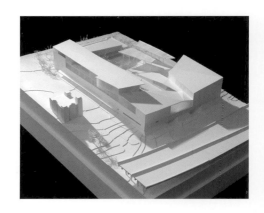

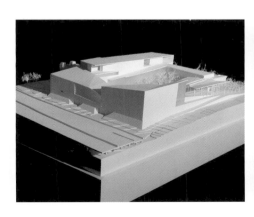 

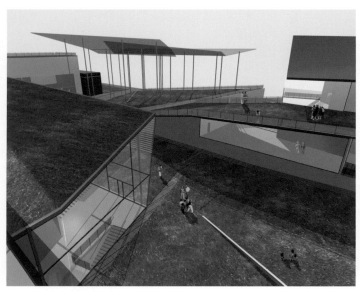

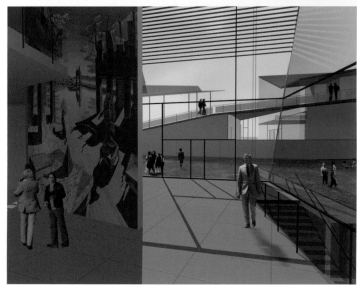

Chilmark House

Martha's Vineyard, Massachusetts, 2001

My colleagues and I have completed nearly a dozen projects on Martha's Vineyard, including a school and The Polly Hill Arboretum Visitors' Center. After we had designed several houses, a couple approached us about designing a small summer home in Chilmark. They owned a gently sloped wooded lot abutting conservation land, with partial views of Vineyard Sound.

Our scheme is highly responsive to the clients' wish for well-defined public and private spaces. In essence, the house can be seen as three moves: a master bedroom wing, a guest wing, and a spacious central room that combines living, dining, and kitchen areas. The public living space, including a sitting area in the guest wing, is oriented to the back of the site and opens to the south and the conservation land. The living area sits between the sun-drenched south and the site's wooded northern edge, allowing in plentiful sunlight and views of the Sound across a quiet road. The approach to the house is by a rustic stone path; entry is into the main living area. Interior elliptical columns and large sliding doors and windows allow walls to disappear and occupants to connect to the landscape. Terraces and a roof deck further heighten the experience of the outdoors; inside, a palette of warm woods temper the modern design. The project continues to evolve: we are presently designing a guesthouse on the property.

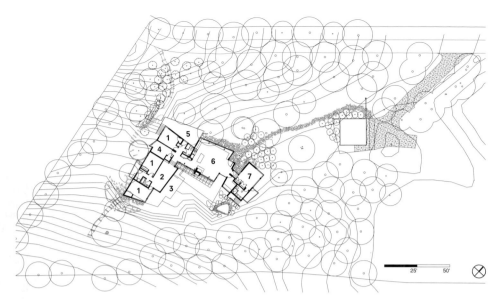

1 Bedroom
2 Sunroom
3 Terrace
4 Bunk room
5 Deck
6 Great room
7 Master bedroom

Site plan

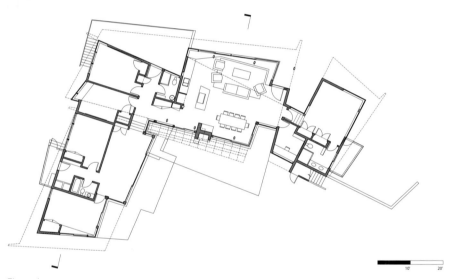

Floor plan

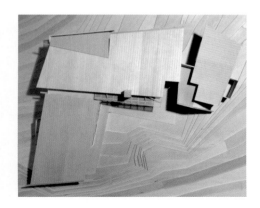

West elevation

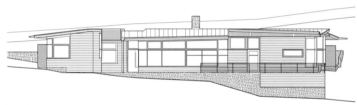

North elevation

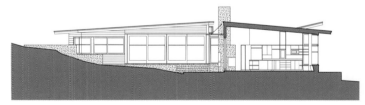

Section looking west

Section looking west

10'   20'

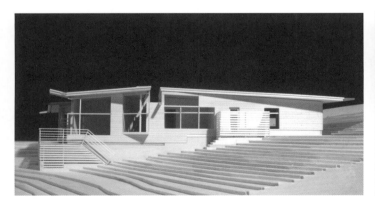

American University of Beirut, School of Business, Competition

Beirut, Lebanon, 2003

We were one of five firms invited to this international competition, which offered a chance to design a new business school for the American University of Beirut on a hillside overlooking the Mediterranean Sea. We approached the project as an opportunity to make a broad gesture to the campus and the city: our design raised the profile of the business school with a complex visible from downtown; it transformed the public edge of the campus by directly linking the new school to Beirut's Corniche; and it sought to enhance the university's landscape tradition.

Given the large space requirements for the school, we chose to break the mass into two straightforward pieces: a sandstone bar and adjacent glass tower, which were connected by a planted bridge. The space between the two structures forms a dramatic portal opening at the courtyard to the Mediterranean; this gesture was inspired in part by a local pattern we observed where many downtown streets are vistas in the dense urban fabric leading to the sea. Our design is oriented to the pure horizon of the sea and uses transparent and perforated skins, which make the sea visible and respond to climate, breezes, and sun positions. The building masses harmonize with the campus and the urbanism of the Corniche, and the simple geometry of the forms echo the distinctive and historic buildings of the campus.

We also included in our design a new organizational plan for the lower part of the campus, of which the School of Business is a part. The large courtyard we proposed is sited along a key north-south pedestrian walkway. We intended the courtyard to serve not only the School of Business but as a new central gathering place for the lower campus. We were struck by how the campus is an oasis in the city. Our landscape designs sought to heighten that sense of a garden retreat. We proposed a variety of outdoor shaded spaces in the form of a large bosque and trellised terraces. The new plaza we recommended is on a plinth adjacent to the Corniche, offering views of the central business district and the distant mountains to the north.

1   Great hall
2   Terrace on Corniche
3   Loading/Parking garage access
4   Conference
5   Reception
6   Mail room
7   Student lounge
8   Cafeteria
9   Study garden

Ground floor plan

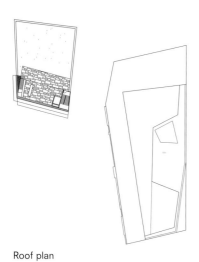

Roof plan

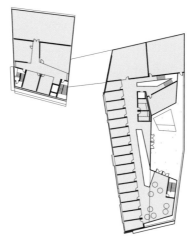

Fifth floor plan

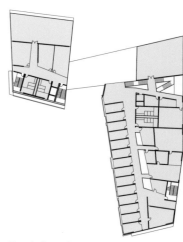

Fourth floor plan

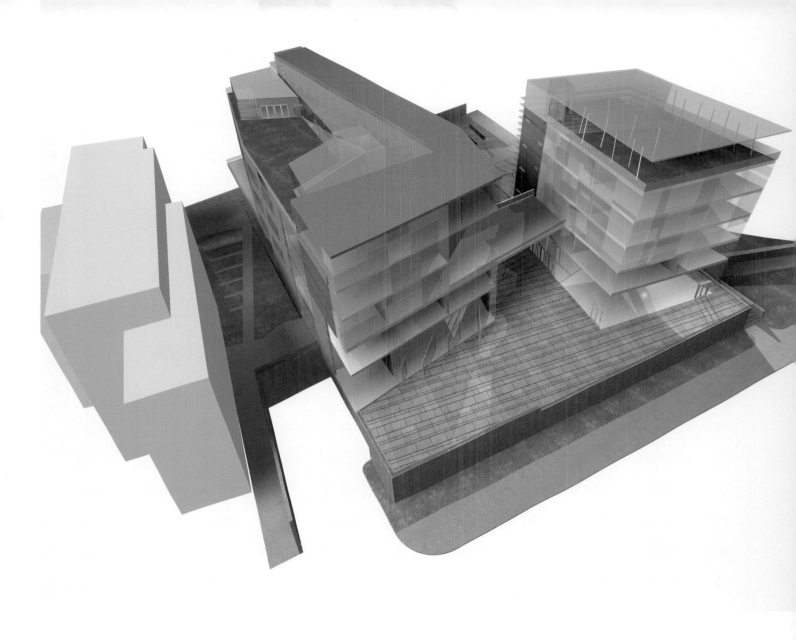

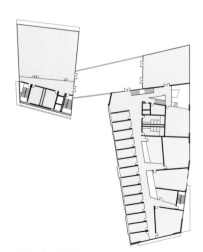

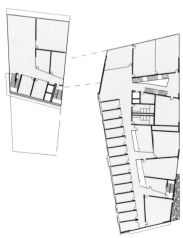

Third floor plan

Second floor p an

Top left: Green space
Top right: Site circulation
Bottom left: Critical views from campus
Bottom right: Views from site

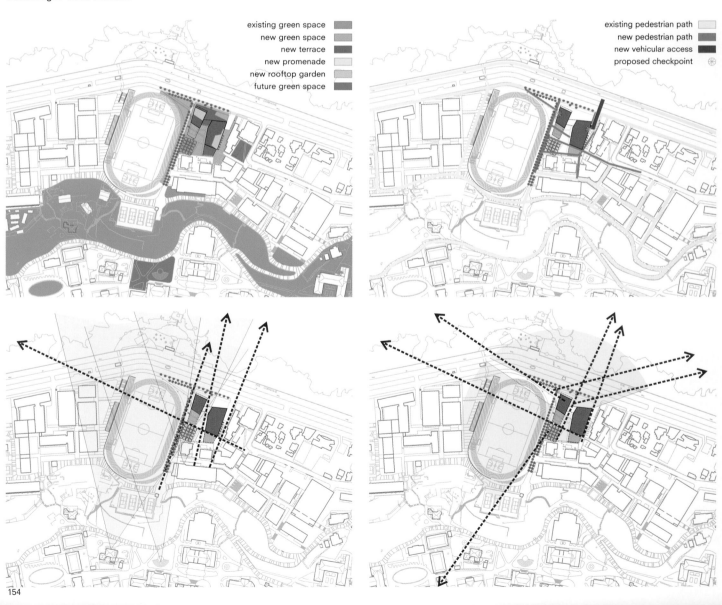

existing green space
new green space
new terrace
new promenade
new rooftop garden
future green space

existing pedestrian path
new pedestrian path
new vehicular access
proposed checkpoint

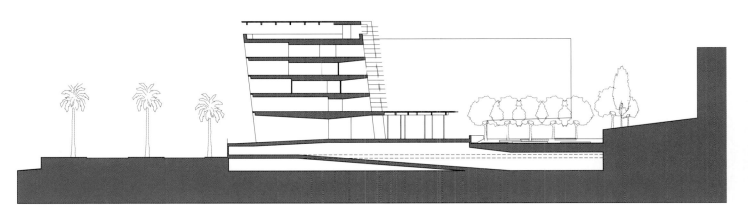

Section looking east

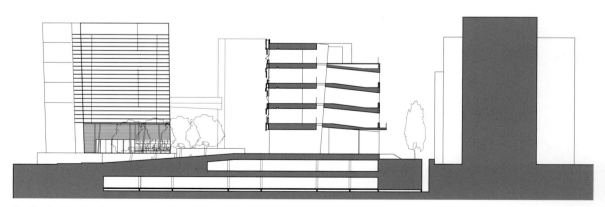

Section looking north

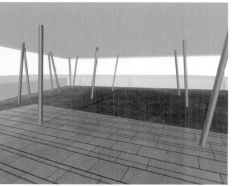

Gloucester House

Gloucester, Massachusetts, 2004

This private residence occupies a granite ledge overlooking the Atlantic Ocean. The ocean perch and oblique slope of the site led us to a design that is markedly different on the land side from the ocean-facing north side. On the land side, the house is low and buffers the wind and salt spray, creating an intimate and protected south-facing courtyard through which visitors approach. Oceanside, the design opens dramatically as the slope drops off, the roof rises like a sail, and the house becomes an observation platform, with an expansive wall of windows three stories high.

One of the house's bolder forms, a large folding roof plane on the western side, acts as a hood that offers shade when the sun is in the southwest. From inside, the sculptural roofline can be traced from the western end to a massive fireplace at the eastern end of the living room. The interior plan is open: the kitchen, dining room, and living room flow into each other; however, the kitchen can be closed off during formal dinners by four sliding steel-and-glass panels.

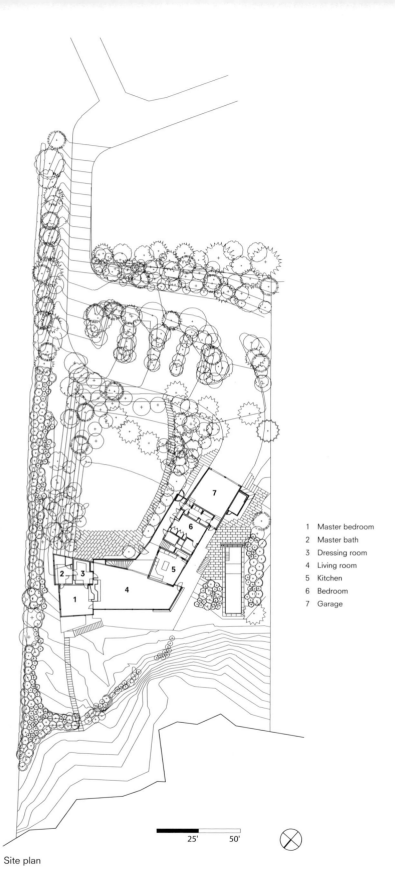

1   Master bedroom
2   Master bath
3   Dressing room
4   Living room
5   Kitchen
6   Bedroom
7   Garage

25'   50'

Site plan

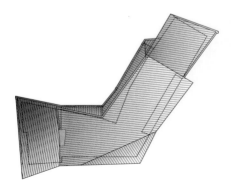

Roof plan

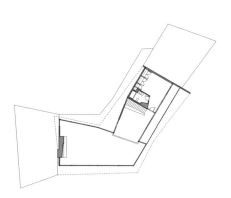

Upper level plan

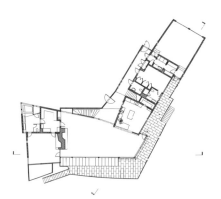

Main level plan

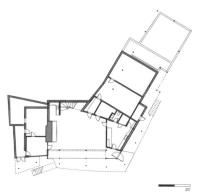

Lower level plan

Northwest elevation

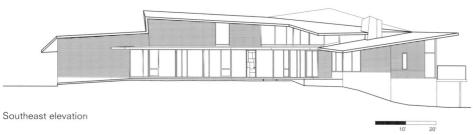

Southeast elevation

10'   20'

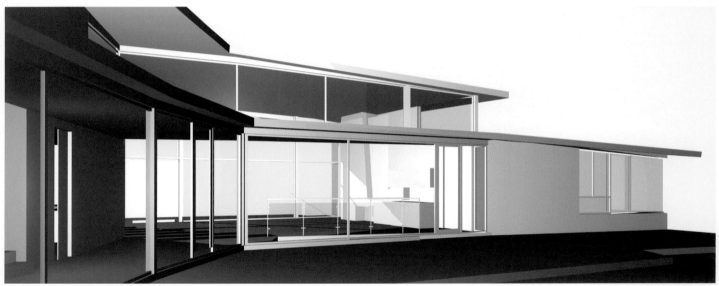

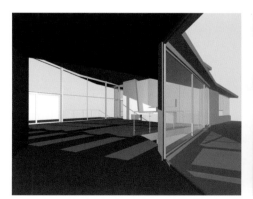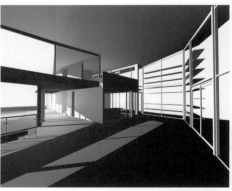

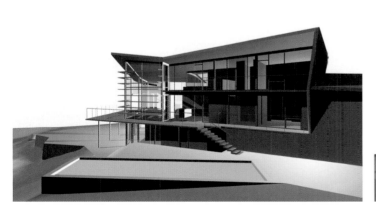

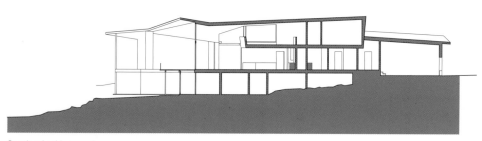

Section looking north

10'   20'

Section looking south

10'   23'

West 22nd Street

New York, New York, 1998

Located within the Chelsea arts district and just west of the High Line, the project is an adaptive reuse of a nineteenth-century light-industrial structure. The building now houses a large retail space on the ground floor, an apartment on the second floor, and a gallery and residence on the upper three floors. We preserved the brick facade and introduced a new structural frame to the fifty-foot by one-hundred-foot lot, which was bounded by brick party walls. The facade preserves the existing streetscape and acts as a foil, concealing the private, open, and contemporary spaces within. In places the facade is fully engaged in the definition of interior space; at other points the facade is detached and becomes an object— a kind of relic that reflects the passing of time.

The residence occupies the uppermost stories, which wrap around a garden on the entry level. The effect of the garden is both delightful and practical: it creates an airy void that opens up to the New York City sky and also reflects the client's desire for outdoor spaces and light-filled interiors. The garden permeates the design: it is the opening through which occupants visually connect to the house's layered spaces, thereby creating a seamless experience of interior and exterior, urban and natural.

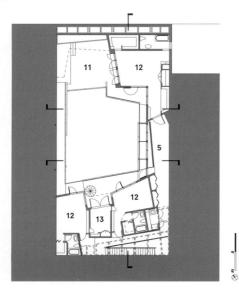

Fourth floor plan

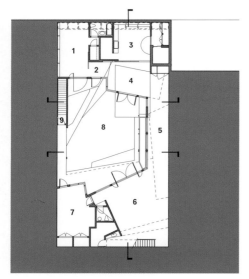

Third floor plan

1 Study
2 Foyer
3 Kitchen
4 Dining area
5 Gallery
6 Living room
7 Family room
8 Garden
9 Entry vestibule
10 Dining terrace
11 Garden terrace
12 Bedroom
13 Playroom

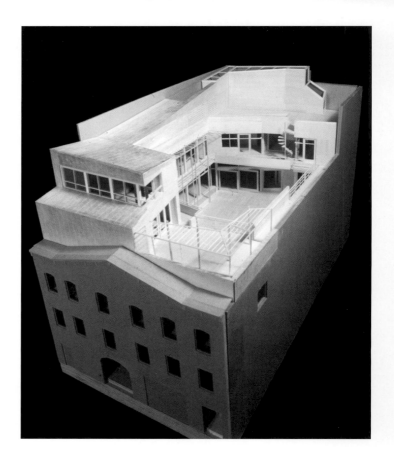

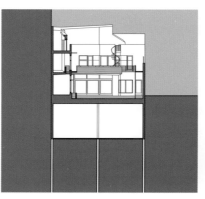

Section looking south

Section looking north

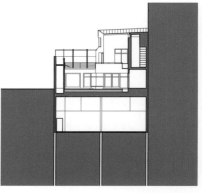

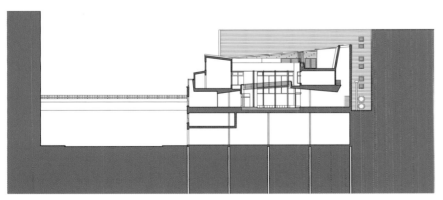

Section looking east

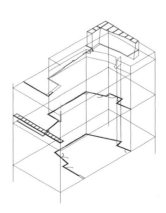

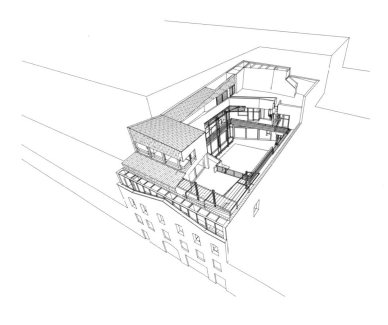

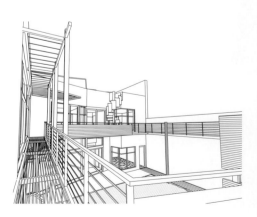

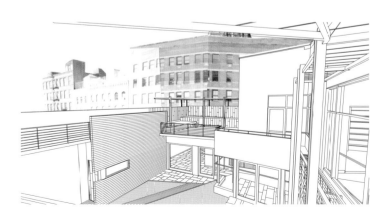

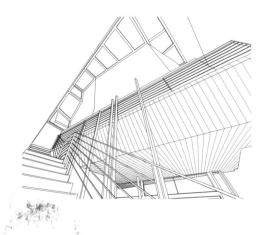

The Work of Charles Rose

Brian Carter

The work of Charles Rose stands apart in the context of contemporary American architecture; while it is clearly preoccupied with the nature of the object and the particularities of site, it strives to reveal deeper understandings of the wider landscape. Developed from a series of modest projects on predominantly rural sites, the buildings designed by Rose now include large and complex educational facilities, galleries, centers for the performing arts, propositions that engage intense urban conditions, and a significant new international gateway.

After completing his studies at Princeton and Harvard universities, Rose worked with the landscape architect Michael Van Valkenburgh before establishing his own practice. Shaped by that experience, he frequently speaks of formulating an architecture that "sees the site." His search, however, not only embraces considerations of site but also looks for inspiration to the work of Le Corbusier, Siza, and Aalto. Recalling their preoccupations with the land and building, it brings to mind Aalto's observation that "nothing old is ever reborn. But it never completely disappears either. And everything that ever has been emerges in a new form."[1]

In searching for new form in the presence of that which "never completely disappears," Rose focuses on the confluence of landscape, site, and building. Camp Paint Rock (2000), a summer camp for underprivileged inner-city teenagers from Los Angeles, is animated by that search. Consisting of a series of modest buildings in Wyoming, it combines considerations of extensive natural systems with the fine details of construction. In establishing the basis for a new settlement in an expansive landscape, Rose first sought to create an appropriate gathering place. Located strategically at the mouth of a canyon, the camp is designed around a series of terraces cut in the ground, centered on two substantial stone hearths and defined by a light timber-framed shelter. In exploring earthwork and frame, this building references the primordial dwelling and those essential forms of construction defined by Semper. In sharp contrast, a series of tiny cabins designed to provide basic shelter has been scattered on the surrounding slopes. Perched on platforms and situated within the trees, they establish a direct connection between the natural and constructed worlds and, by overlooking the canyon, clearly recognize the omnipresence of the landscape. At the same time, these "flying" fragments leave that landscape virtually

1. Alvar Aalto, "'Painters and masons," *Jousimies*, 1921, in *Alvar Aalto, 1898–1976*, ed. Aarno Ruusvuori and Juhani Pallasma (Helsinki: Museum of Finnish Architecture, 1978), 69.

untouched. The emphatic distinctions between group and individual, heavy and light, rational and whimsical, at Camp Paint Rock create a group of buildings that successfully establishes a new community in this place and, at the same time, provides a basis for young people of the city to comprehend a vast, new, and unfamiliar world.

While their siting is informed by readings of the landscape, these fragments have been shaped by other characteristics of the place. Reflecting the architect's curiosity about landform and weather and their impact on construction, the cabins take on original and often surprising traits as they twist to lean into the wind, tilt to catch rainwater, open up to take in the sun, and fold in ways that create eccentric but effective shelters.

However, the work of Charles Rose is not an architecture that merely seeks to provide shelter or reflect on a search for stasis. It provokes movement. At Camp Paint Rock, this provocation projects movement beyond simple connections between buildings. Networks of elevated boardwalks, footpaths, and horseback-riding trails offer different readings of the place, and, in reinterpreting the promenade, Rose has been able to create experiential sequences that order the site through a series of carefully composed views. In these sequences, the buildings that he has designed, both at Camp Paint Rock and elsewhere, appear to evolve and change along these contrived routes where they seem to be "emerging from the earth."[2]

The body of work also demonstrates an aggressive pursuit of the development of form through rigorous explorations of construction. At a time when manufacturing processes and construction systems are increasingly being deployed to save time and consequently replace craft, Rose sets up resistance. A deep appreciation for sound building, shaped by a thorough understanding of materials and traditional construction techniques, clearly underpins his approach to design. In several projects, this has resulted in an inspired use of wood and an impressive precision in the detail of its assembly. In the Orleans House on Cape Cod (2004), construction systems are made explicit and the details of cladding and connections conspicuously refined. Parts of the building, like the office tower, which have been transformed into totemic elements that prompt ways of moving across the site, are also made with extraordinary care. Similarly, external wood screens and finely detailed moveable panels, designed to provide shade and offer privacy, become intimately

2. Karen D. Stein, "Projects," Architectural Record, June 1998, 107.

scaled pieces of refined construction that create moments of intensity within a larger whole.

In the design of public buildings, these considerations of material and detailing of constructional systems have been directed to explore a broader range of ideas relative to building and landscape. So while Rose's design for the new campus center at Brandeis University (2002) pursues the use of stone as a response to nearby orthogonal modernist pavilions, the new skins of fossilized limestone that he has developed are also assertively sculpted in ways that recall the rocky outcroppings that define the more expansive natural setting of this particular campus.

In this project, Rose has created a series of communal rooms at the heart of the building that underlines the vitality of student life and at the same time transforms the building into an observatory with panoramic views out across the campus. Together with competition designs for the American University of Beirut and the Booker T. Washington High School in Dallas, the Gulf Coast Museum of Art (2001), and the new Business School at The University of South Dakota (expected completion, 2008), this work projects Rose's design contribution emphatically beyond the private world of the house into the public domain of the campus and the city.

These commissions to design larger and more complex buildings, coupled with the prescriptive demands of institutional clients, have encouraged the development of new ways of working. Collaborations with technical specialists, including Arup and Buro Happold, are furthering studies of materials, passive systems, and structure to expand the intuitive responses that inspired earlier projects. The Currier Center for the Performing Arts at The Putney School (2004), with its sheltering forms backed up to the edge of an existing forest, advances a range of ideas related to the development of a distinctly rural campus. By planning an ambitious range of new civic spaces under a series of folded and planted roofs, it clearly acknowledges its setting while furthering ideas of sustainability that qualify the center for LEED certification.

Rose's proposal for the United States Port of Entry in Del Rio, Texas, (2004) developed under the U. S. General Services Administration's Design Excellence Program, defines an important threshold on the international border between the United States and Mexico.

Located in the harsh environment of western Texas, the design effectively combines the ingenuity of the vernacular with ideas developed through focused research, interdisciplinary work, and the rigorous testing of prototypes. Within a new landscape created by the construction of an extensive infrastructure, sweeping canopies form generous and welcome shaded spaces that define a particularly appropriate version of this increasingly important architectural type. Working closely with engineers, the detailed design of the structure and cladding of these canopies has been developed to emphasize lightness yet also induce passive ventilation. At the same time, a collection of buildings sheltered by these canopies benefits from plentiful but carefully filtered natural light and has been planned around a series of enclosed gardens that in turn encourage evaporative cooling. These informed design moves will clearly improve the quality of the workplace for staff and create a necessary moment of calm for travelers moving between these two countries.

Rose has spoken of "creating an architecture that stands in relationship to its surroundings, heightens the experience of the natural conditions at work in the setting, and focuses, orients, and reorients one's perception of the land through the nature of the constructed object." This is an approach that is in stark contrast to many current architectural preoccupations with self-indulgent form making, the digital toolbox and building skin. By focusing on the nature, character, and perception of the land, Charles Rose is not only discovering but actively demonstrating other and arguably more profound ways of creating modern architecture and defining place.

Leeper Studio Complex,
Atlantic Center for the Arts

New Smyrna Beach, Florida, 1997

Set in a dense ecological preserve on Florida's Intracoastal Waterway, the complex serves a renowned artists' residency program. We designed new studios for dance, drama, painting, sculpture, and music, as well as a black-box theater, a library, and a dining hall. Studio pavilions and buildings are woven into the dense vegetation, creating a sense of complete immersion into the landscape. The pavilions are linked by a boardwalk that sits two and a half feet off the jungle floor. The boardwalk is primarily a path for circulation, but it often becomes a place for chance encounters and the exchange of ideas between collaborating artists.

Carriage House

St. David's, Pennsylvania, 2004

Located on a gentle slope within a mature landscape, this outbuilding serves several purposes: it is a gatehouse along a drive to a large residential complex; it is a garage displaying three unique, high-performance automobiles; it is an office for the grounds manager; and it houses a collection of arts and crafts objects and paintings. Natural light permeates the interiors through clerestories located at the juncture of the sculptural volumes that form the building. The upper floor is clad in wood and copper; the lower floor is made of stone. Light trellises made of acid-washed stainless steel will be planted with trailing vines. West of the building, a planar sculpture court is terraced into the site. A stone motor court provides access to a footpath that leads to the main house.

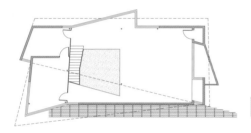
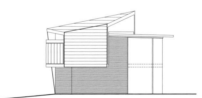

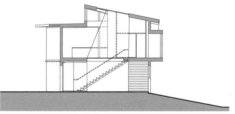
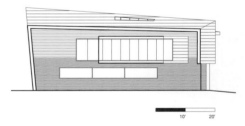

School of Business,
The University of South Dakota

Vermillion, South Dakota, 2005

The building design powerfully organizes The University of South Dakota campus by establishing a landscape that connects the currently disjointed northern and southern ends with a newly defined quadrangle and path system. The site plan creates new vistas on campus, locates an outdoor classroom for both the business school and the broader campus community, and provides an organizing landscape that in turn designates sites for future university buildings.

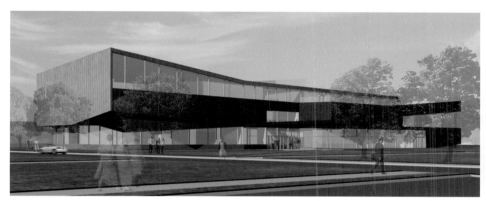

Westport House

Westport, Massachusetts, 2004

Sited on an expansive, riverfront lot, the house is positioned on a bluff at the edge of a natural clearing and oriented to optimize river views. Clerestory windows created by sloping, shifting roof planes introduce abundant natural light throughout the two-story residence. An energy-efficient geothermal system heats and cools the house.

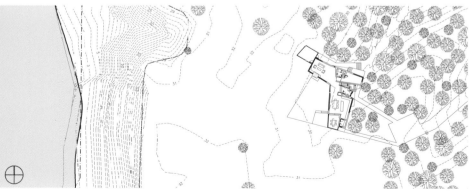

Charlton College of Business, University of Massachusetts

Dartmouth, Massachusetts, 2004

The Charlton College of Business is the first structure to be added to the University of Massachusetts's Dartmouth campus since Paul Rudolf designed its buildings in the 1970s. The size of the new building is small in comparison to the massive and connected volumes of the original brutalist structures. With an existing library, the College of Business frames a new south-facing open space. Resting on a precast concrete base, the college is a blocklike cantilevered bar—a counterweight to the active, sculptural facades of Rudolf's buildings.

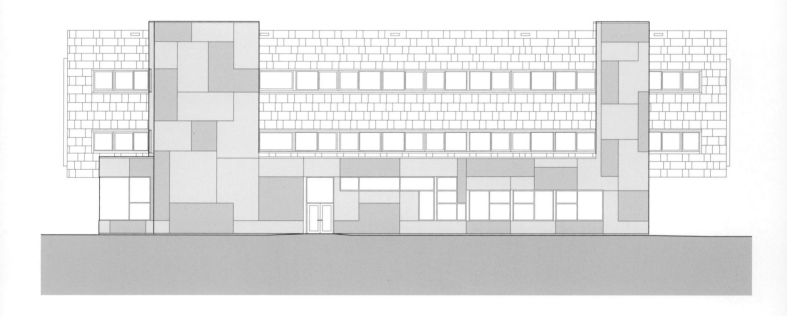

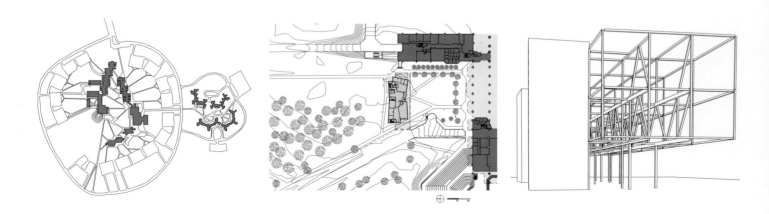

Temple Beth Am, Competition

Miami, Florida, 1999

This project comprises an elementary school, a large sanctuary and social hall, an intimate chapel, and a library. Landscapes include a chapel water garden and a garden memorializing the Holocaust. The design strives to inspire a palpable experience of the spiritual through the interplay of architecture and landscape, the symbolic use of water and light, and a spatial progression through the site that unfolds gradually, evoking life's journey. In the sanctuary a series of stained glass panels of bulrushes signify the salvation of Moses. The inter-weaving of landscape and architecture and the creation of carefully controlled views enhance the meditative quality of the temple complex.

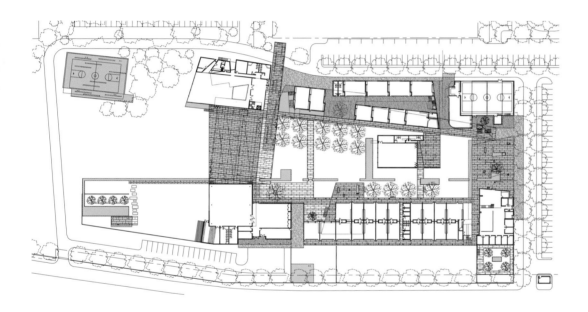

Amphitheater and Bathhouse

Acton, Massachusetts, 1999

The amphitheater and bathhouse are located within a reclaimed forty-acre quarry, two miles north of the historic town center. The terraced site is surrounded by forest and centered on an artificial pond. Approached from the south, the bathhouse serves as a gateway to the beach and amphitheater. The bathhouse includes an office, concession stand, and an outdoor terrace. The amphitheater is made of a massive semicircular berm with an elevated promenade and pigmented concrete stage covered by an oversized roof.

Center for the Arts

Longboat Key, Florida, 1999

The center is a collection of studios and exhibition spaces for local artists. By closing a road that had bifurcated the site, we reoriented existing structures around a central landscape. Two new buildings were designed as part of the project: a gallery and a large studio. We also renovated a multipurpose room and offices. The new scheme seamlessly weaves these disparate architectural elements into a coherent architectural and landscape design.

 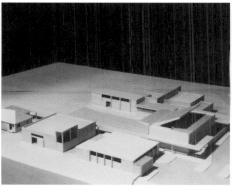 

Gulf Coast Museum of Art, Florida Botanical Garden

Largo, Florida, Phases 1-3: 1999; Phases 4-6: 2001

The Gulf Coast Museum blends a flexible exhibition space for a growing regional art collection with studio workshops and classrooms for a community arts-education program and offices for the Gulf Coast Art Center. The museum is also part of a cultural complex: the Florida Botanical Garden, which the museum is woven into; Pinellas Historical Museum; and Heritage Village, an open-air exhibit of "cracker" architecture. The museum defines a boundary between the botanical gardens and Pinellas waterway, on the other side of which is Heritage Village. Two circulation elements organize the project: a sinuous colonnade running parallel to the waterway and a footbridge across the wetlands that connects the museum to Heritage Village. The public center of the complex—with an auditorium, library, café, sculpture garden, galleries, and the museum store—is at the intersection of these two paths. North-facing skylights give the roof a distinctive form and diffuse the sun's rays. The interior glows with natural light.

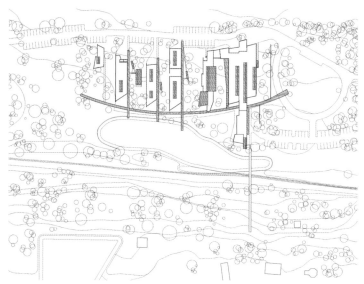

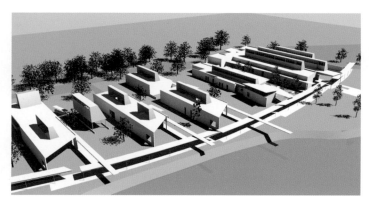

Woodland Dormitories, Kenyon College

Gambier, Ohio, 1993

We worked intensively with a student design team to find a site for this four-building dormitory complex. The sloped, wooded site is next to Old Kenyon, a Gothic hulk and the original college building that anchors the eastern end of Kenyon's notable mile-long axis, around which the school is organized. The dorm site extends the axis and is woven into the college's formal plan of organization. This approach respects the planning traditions of the historic campus and establishes a loosely defined courtyard framed by four "object" buildings. Entry to each dorm is from the courtyard.

Earth Science Building, Kimberton Waldorf School

Kimberton, Pennsylvania, 2001

Part of a phased master plan, the classroom building supports a unique gardening and earth sciences program at this Pennsylvania farm school. The design provides space for experimenting, writing, and drawing—activities integral to the Waldorf curriculum.

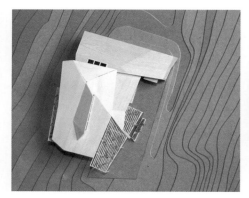 

Friends School

Mullica Hill, New Jersey, 2001

We were asked to design a middle school for an expanding Quaker school in southwestern New Jersey. The building was to be the first developed in the school's master plan, which organized a central sloping lawn flanked by buildings to the north and south. The lawn was centered on the existing Mullica Hill Friends Meetinghouse, a building adjacent to the school site that served the Friends community. The simplicity of the building reflects the frugal philosophy of the school.

 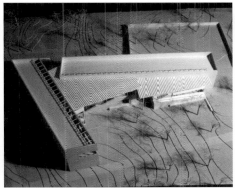 

Global Offices, Gemini Consulting

Cambridge, Massachusetts; Oslo, Norway; Johannesburg, South Africa; London, England, 1997

Gemini, an international management consulting firm, commissioned Wellington Reiter and Charles Rose to design a 35,000-square-foot prototypical "office of the future" in Cambridge, Massachusetts. The project served as a prototype for Gemini offices globally and led to projects in Oslo, London, and Johannesburg. The design challenges conventional notions of traditional office structures and re-imagines Gemini's office as a nonterritorial, nonhierarchical "home base," with both actual and virtual support services and workspaces for office-based staff and Gemini's mobile field consultants.

Headquarters, International Fund for Animal Welfare

Yarmouth, Massachusetts, 2001

The International Fund for Animal Welfare (IFAW) aims to reduce commercial exploitation of animals, protect wildlife habitats, and help animals in distress. Our design for the nonprofit's global headquarters on Cape Cod puts a premium on environmental sensitivity and energy efficiency. The building will house information displays about IFAW's worldwide projects, a 200-seat conference center and auditorium, and offices for headquarters and visiting staff.

The building was designed to garner the highest LEED rating. Features and systems include on-site wastewater treatment and passive solar design. The building's massing and orientation, and window size, location, and shading, were designed to maximize efficient energy use. Trellises shade summer sun, while a system of light shelves reflects daylight deep into the building. Among the recycled building materials are steel for the structure, carpets, gypsum wallboard, and rapidly renewable bamboo for floors. Occupancy sensors, light sensors, and automatic dimmers further increase energy efficiency.

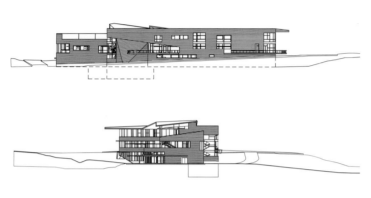

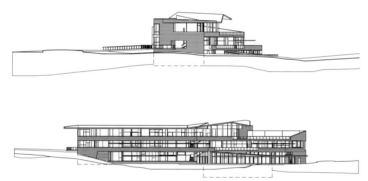

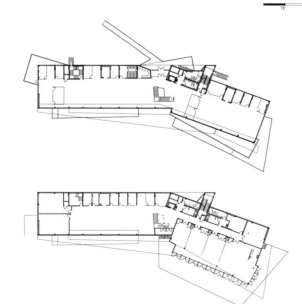

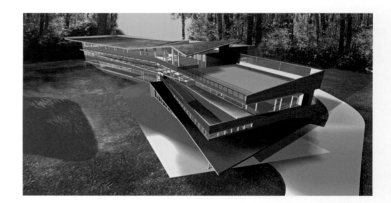

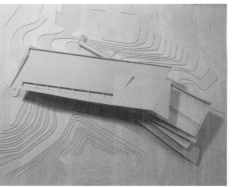
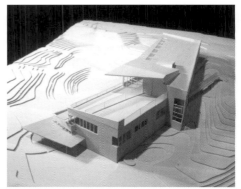

The Hartsbrook School

Hadley, Massachusetts, 1990

The Hartsbrook School is a Waldorf school, which uses an international teaching method drawing on the spiritualism and philosophy of Rudolf Steiner. Arts, crafts, music, and an emphasis on educating the "whole child" are essential parts of the Hartsbrook School's teaching approach. Our Hartsbrook master plan sites seven buildings in a field in relation to features in the surrounding farmland. One has been built; a second is under way.

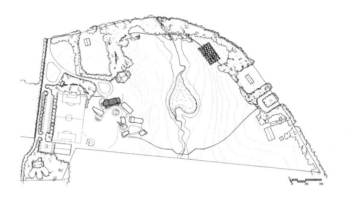

Bluff House

Martha's Vineyard, Massachusetts, 1999

Screened from the street by a grove of twisted cedars, the large gabled form of the house rises from a ridge that runs through the site. Oceanside, the house has large, curving banks of windows on the ground and second floors that take in views of Vineyard Sound and the Atlantic Ocean. The design is directly influenced by the Arts and Crafts movement. Interior materials include stone floors, murals, waxed walls, highly crafted timber beams, and a dark, richly toned oak staircase.

Visitors' Center, The Polly Hill Arboretum

Martha's Vineyard, Massachusetts, 1998

The Visitors' Center nestles into the existing woodlands of The Polly Hill Arboretum. The two buildings house a multipurpose visitors' center and public restrooms. A trellis, topped with native locust boughs, links the two structures. Movable furniture allows the center to function as a gift shop during the day and as a meeting room for lectures and presentations during the evening.

Jonathan Nelson Fitness Center at the Erickson Athletic Complex, Brown University, Competition

Providence, Rhode Island, 2005

The core campus of Brown University is a unique weaving of topography, active city streets, gardens, civic landscapes, and historic architecture of intimate scale. The over-sized buildings that comprise the Erickson Athletic complex are disjointed from the landscape, each other, and the street. The design for the Jonathan Nelson Fitness Center establishes a portal to the complex by siting the building along the edge of Hope Street in order to create a large courtyard in the center of the existing athletic complex. The siting diminishes the scale and visual presence of the existing athletic facilities and parking, activates the street edge, and creates a green space characteristic of Brown but responding to the particular scale of its surroundings.

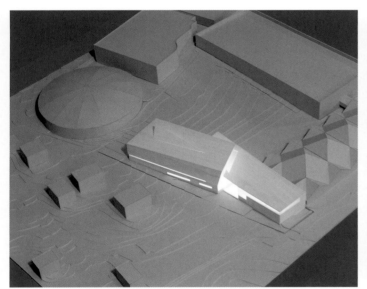
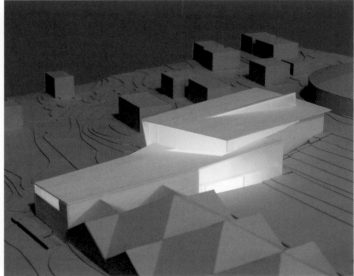

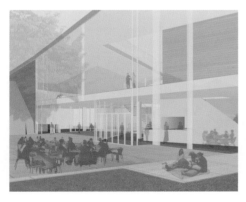

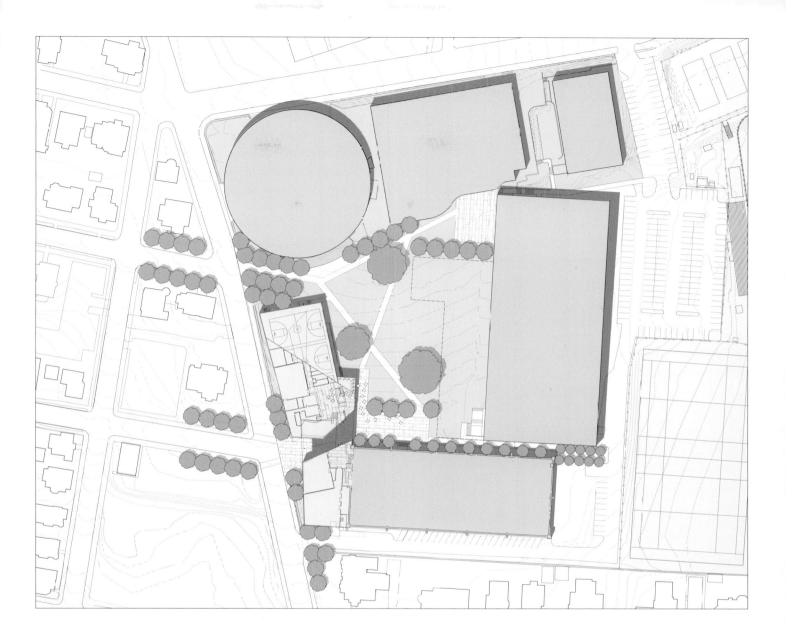

Interdisciplinary Studio, The MacDowell Colony

Peterborough, New Hampshire, 2001

Founded in 1907, The MacDowell Colony has long been known for granting writers, composers, visual artists, photographers, and other artists a solitary haven to pursue their work in one of its thirty-two studios. A growing number of nontraditional artists expressed a need for an interdisciplinary studio—a first for the colony. Designed for up to ten artists at a time, the studio functions as a highly adaptable, multimedia, black-box collaborative space, suitable for choreography, performance art, light and sound exhibitions, and other emerging art forms.

Overhead, a tension-wire grid allows lighting designers to work easily and safely. Natural light can be controlled through a system of mechanized black-out shades. The studio interior opens to the outdoors, where a series of concrete and stone planes create additional performance space. Designed as a wood-and-steel-frame building, the exterior walls will be sheathed in hemlock bark siding; the interior studio walls will be cork panels. As a counterpoint to the collaborative space, a writer's studio defines the south end of the site. The project is sited within a clearing, formerly a corridor for power lines, which have been removed.

  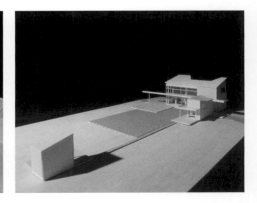

New York Anthroposophical Society

New York, New York, 2002

This renovation transforms an existing five-story, twenty-five-foot-wide row house into the New York branch of the Anthroposophical Society of America. The ground floor includes a library, bookstore, and coffee shop facing north and a large public space on the rear of the building facing south and opening onto a garden. Undulating ceiling forms extend from front to back and are randomly interrupted by vertical partition walls.

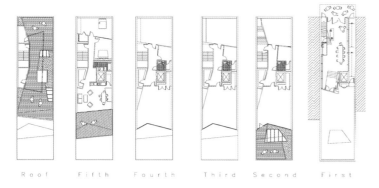

Roof   Fifth   Fourth   Third   Second   First

Office for a Private Investor

Bedminster, New Jersey, 1998

This "home-office" proposes a playful environment that resists conventional notions of what an office is. The existing house acts as a foil to the office addition. The design facilitates informal interaction among occupants.

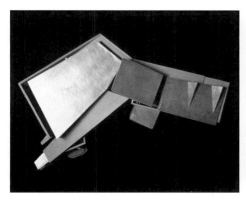

Equipment Shed

San Juan Island, Washington, 1995

Situated on a farm overlooking the Strait of Juan de Fuca, the cedar-clad shed relies on the timber-frame tradition of the Northwest in the service of an expressive, sculptural architecture. The L-shaped configuration of the building deflects the prevailing winds and shelters the adjacent work yard, a square gravel court defined by the building and a tall slatted wood fence. The shed houses the farm office, workspace for a veterinarian, wood and machine shops, and extensive storage space for heavy equipment. Located in a natural clearing at the edge of a dense stand of fir trees, the structure is intimately connected with the farm's windswept landscape, which gives it a dynamic, almost shape-shifting quality when viewed from different points.

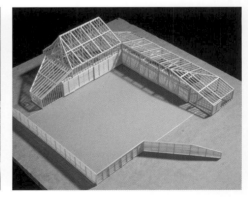

The Foote School

New Haven, Connecticut, 2001

The Foote School occupies half of a city block in suburban New Haven. The school buildings date from the 1950s and the 1960s. Our interventions, which included a gym, an art and music building, and a black-box theater, provides space for a robust arts and theater curriculum. The interventions also serve to formally define the exterior landscape spaces of the school. The new structures are small in scale; their forms compliment the original volumes of the school.

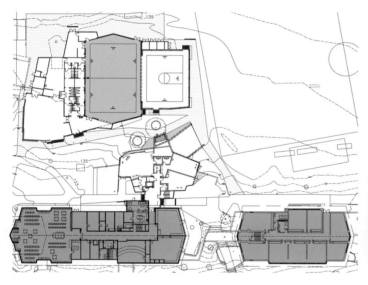

Bartholomew County Veterans Memorial

Columbus, Indiana, 1997

Situated at the entry to Columbus, on the Bartholomew County Courthouse Square, the memorial is a grid with twenty-five limestone pillars honoring soldiers from Bartholomew County who died in twentieth-century wars. With its rough, rock-cut limestone exterior, the memorial appears from a distance as a monolithic block. Up close, it is a thicket of columns, which creates a haven for meditation. Etched on the smooth column surfaces are the veterans' names; letters and diary entries are inscribed on interior columns. At night, lights embedded in the memorial's base create a dramatic play of light and shadow and illuminate the columns' inner surfaces.

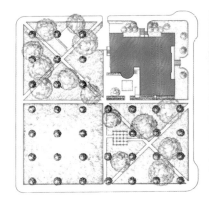
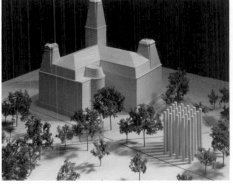

Aquinnah House

Martha's Vineyard, Massachusetts, 1998

A windswept, rolling terrain overlooking Vineyard Sound is the site of this modest vacation "camp." Compressed passageways between simple volumes frame exquisite vistas of the water beyond. The floor elevations shift with the contours of the site. Windows are strategically placed to create dynamic visual connections between the interiors and the site. A roof platform offers panoramic views of Aquinnah Light, the Sound, and Woods Hole.

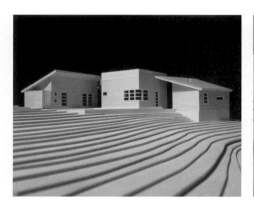

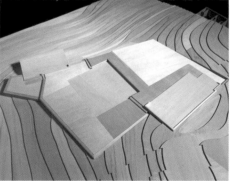

Acknowledgments

I wish to thank Princeton Architectural Press and the Graham Foundation for the Advanced Studies in the Fine Arts for their warm reception of my work and for their very generous backing, without which this book would not be possible. Clients Alison and John Ferring, David and Betsy Epstein, and John and Carolyn Alm also provided generous financial support, and I am indebted to them. Over the years, Kevin Lippert has published a group of remarkable books that have made a significant contribution to the understanding of architecture, and I am grateful to him for publishing a monograph of my work.

I am very fortunate to have worked with extraordinary clients; they have become important friends and mentors to me. My special thanks and appreciation goes to Alison and John Ferring, Diane and Sam Bodman, John and Carolyn Alm (and camp kudos!), Kate Ganz, Sarah Gray Gund, Carl and Ruth Shapiro, Ronnie and Michael Zinner, Jehuda Reinharz, Peter French, Terry and Susan Ragon, David and Betsy Epstein, Michael Weinstein, Fan and Donald Ogilvie, Ted Potter, Suzanne Fetscher, Art and Heide Zajonc, Joan Shafran and Rob Haimes, Ken Rollins, Alan Plattus, David Teiger, Brian Morgan, Randall Smith, David and Joan Smith, Cheryl Young, Craig Bradley, and Bob and Happy Doran.

Over the years, so many talented and exceptional architects have worked in my office; in particular, I wish to thank Eric Robinson and Heather Weiss for their dedication, their remarkable work on projects in this book, and their endurance!

Brian Carter hired me in 1998 as a guest critic at the University of Michigan, and I greatly appreciate his understanding of my work, his support, and the essay he has contributed to this book. Terrence Riley and I served on an architectural awards jury several years ago, and I came away with great admiration for his gifts of insight and rigorous analysis. I am delighted that he wrote the introduction for this book. Most of the images in this book were taken by two outstanding American photographers, Chuck Choi and John Edward Linden; thank you for your superb work. Susi Sanchez, Melissa Bland, and Mason Pritchett, designers at Charles Rose Architects, were instrumental in preparing the monograph images. The monstrous job of organizing this material—culling a few hundred images from more than four thousand—fell to Jeremy Voorhees, and I owe him a big thanks.

The work shown here reflects my career to date. I could not have accomplished what I have without the help of Peter Waldman, who is responsible for encouraging me to pursue architecture when I was an undergraduate at Princeton University. Long after I left Princeton, he remained a valued mentor. Others who helped me develop as an architect are Raphael Moneo, Denise Scott Brown, Moshe Safdie, Michael Van Valkenburgh, Michael Graves, and Stephen Harris. Three other teachers from my past need mention: Ekkehard Piening was a dear friend who helped me believe in myself; Susl Berlin, my teacher for eight years at the Waldorf School, demanded excellence, taught holistically, and brought insight and intensity to my education; and Rosetta Goodkind from whom I learned so much about quality and refinement.

My parents, George and Faith Rose, deserve a special award for their attendance at many building dedications and their permissive attitude toward my early backyard construction projects. Thank you, Mom and Dad! My children are some of the best architectural critics I will ever know, and I thank them for their companionship, strong ideas, and willingness to explore this field with me.

Most of all, I wish to thank Pam Moore, my dearest companion and most ardent supporter. She has helped me with this work in countless ways. I dedicate this book to her.

Charles Rose
April 2005

Project Credits

Orleans House
Charles Rose Architects, Inc.: Charles Rose, Design Principal; David Gabriel, Lori Sang, Heather Weiss, Donna Ficca, Karl Erik Larson, Marios Christodoulides; *Landscape Architect*: Stephen Stimson Associates, Inc.; *Structural Engineers*: Arup; *Steel Fabrications*: Rich Corner; *Furnishings*: Haynes Roberts Inc.; *Contractor*: Scott Sisson.

Carl and Ruth Shapiro Campus Center, Brandeis University
Charles Rose Architects, Inc.: Charles Rose, Design Principal; Jim Moore, Project Architect; *Landscape Architect*: Stephen Stimson Associates, Inc.; *Civil Engineer*: Judith Nitsch Engineering, Inc.; *Consulting Engineers*: Arup; *Theater Consultant*: Alan P. Symonds; *Acoustics*: Acentech; *Code*: R.W. Sullivan; *Specifications*: David Lund; *Signage*: Whitney Veigas; *Construction Manager*: Berry.

Currier Center for the Performing Arts, The Putney School
Charles Rose Architects, Inc.: Charles Rose, Design Principal; Heather Weiss, Project Architect; Lori Sang, Marios Christodoulides, David Whitney, Helena Hallman, Melissa Bland; *Structural Engineer*: Richmond So Engineers; *Consulting Mechanical Engineers*: Kohler and Lewis; *Code*: R.W. Sullivan; *Specifications*: David Lund; *Acoustics*: Acentech, Carl Rosenberg; *Theater*: Alan P. Symonds; *Construction Manager*: DEW Construction.

Copper House
Charles Rose Architects, Inc.: Charles Rose, Design Principal; Heather Weiss, Marios Christodoulides, Karl Eric Larson, Pam Moore; *Structural Engineer*: Richmond So Engineers; *Contractor*: EAC Construction, Rico Colangeli, Principal; *Furniture*: Charles Rose Architects, Inc.: Charles Rose, Pam Moore, Susi Sanchez.

United States Port of Entry
Charles Rose Architects, Inc.: Charles Rose, Design Principal; Eric Robinson, Project Architect; Susi Sanchez, Mason Pritchett, Heather Weiss, Melissa Bland; *Structural Engineering*: Datum Gojer Engineers, LLC; *Landscape Architects*: SWA Group; *Civil Engineering*: Brown Engineering Co.; *Mechanical Engineering*: BLW Engineers, Inc.; *Cost*: Hanscomb Faithful & Gould; *Code*: Rolf Jensen & Associates, Inc.

Camp Paint Rock
Charles Rose Architects, Inc.: Charles Rose, Design Principal; Eric Robinson, David Gabriel, David Martin, Project Architects; *Design Team*: Charles Rose, Maryann Thompson, Franco Ghiraldi, Marios Christodoulides, David Martin, Takashi Yanai, Chris Hoxie, Lori Sang, Heide Beebe; Samantha Pearson, Patricia Chen; *Structural Engineers*: Arup; *Consulting Engineers*: Patterson, Weber and Associates; *Civil Engineer*: Dick Steedly; *Contractor*: Groathouse Construction, Inc.

Booker T. Washington High School for the Performing and Visual Arts, Competition
Charles Rose Architects, Inc.: Charles Rose, Design Principal; Eric Robinson, Project Architect; Marios Christodoulides, Lori Sang, David Gabriel, Jim Moore, Donna Ficca, Karl Erik Larson; *Consulting Engineers*: Arup.

Chilmark House
Charles Rose Architects, Inc., formerly Thompson and Rose Architects: Charles Rose, Principal-in-Charge; Eric Robinson, Project Architect; *Design Team*: Charles Rose, Maryann Thompson, Eric Robinson, Franco Ghiraldi. *Landscape Architect*: Michael Van Valkenburgh Associates, Inc.; *Structural Engineer*: Ocmulgee Associates, Inc.; *Contractor*: Hodson/Steele Inc.

American University of Beirut, School of Business, Competition
Charles Rose Architects, Inc.: Charles Rose, Design Principal; Jim Moore, Project Architect; Marios Chritodoulides, Eric Robinson, Heather Weiss; *Consulting Engineer*: Arup; *Cost Consultant*: Hanscomb Faithful & Gould.

Gloucester House
Charles Rose Architects, Inc.: Charles Rose, Design Principal; Heather Weiss, David Whitney, Helena Hallman, Patricia Chen; *Interiors*: Saffron House; *Landscape Architect*: Michael Van Valkenburgh Associates, Inc.; *Structural Engineering*: Richmond So Engineers; *Contractor*: Thoughtforms Corporation.

West 22nd Street
Charles Rose Architects, Inc.: Charles Rose, Design Principal; Lori Sang, Project Architect; *Design Team*: Charles Rose, Maryann Thompson, Lori Sang, Chris Hoxie, Franco Ghiraldi, Heide Beebe, Takashi Yanai; *Landscape Architect*: Thomas Balsley Associates; *Structural Engineer*: Georgeopolis Engineers; *Consulting Engineers*: Reynaldo C. Prego Consulting Engineers; *Contractor*: Higgens Construction.

Additional Projects

Leeper Studio Complex
Thompson and Rose Architects, now Charles Rose Architects, Inc.

Carriage House
Charles Rose Architects, Inc.: Charles Rose, Design Principal; Susi Sanchez, Project Designer; Mason Pritchett; *Landscape Architect*: Stephen Stimson Associates, Inc.; *Structural Engineer*: Richmond So Engineers.

School of Business, The University of South Dakota

Charles Rose Architects, Inc.: Charles Rose, Design Principal; Eric Robinson, Project Architect; Marios Christodoulides, Heather Weiss, Patricia Chen, Helena Hallman, Karl Erik Larson, Lori Sang; *Landscape Architect*: Michael Van Valkenburgh Associates, Inc.

Westport House

Charles Rose Architects, Inc.: Heather Weiss, Project Architect; Rob Haimes, Project Designer; Charles Rose, Susi Sanchez; *Structural Engineer*: Richmond So Engineers; *Contractor*: GF Rhode Construction.

Charlton School of Business, University of Massachusetts

Charles Rose Architects, Inc.: Charles Rose, Design Principal; Eric Robinson, Project Architect; Jim Moore, Marios Christodoulides, Patricia Chen, Melissa Bland; *Structural Engineer*: Richmond So Engineers; *Mechanical Engineer*: BLW Engineers, Inc.; *Civil Engineer*: Judith Nitsch Engineering, Inc.; *Contractor*: Bond Brothers Construction; *Owner's Representatives*: Joslin, Lesser & Associates, Inc. University Representative: William Heaney.

Temple Beth Am, Competition

Thompson and Rose Architects, Inc., now Charles Rose Architects, Inc.

Amphitheater and Bathhouse

Thompson and Rose Architects, Inc., now Charles Rose Architects, Inc.; *Structural Engineer*: LY Consulting Engineers, Inc. Uy Thanh Ly, Principal; *Mechanical Engineer*: Erdman Anthony, Consulting Engineers; *Cost Estimators*: Hanscomb Faithful & Gould; *Contractor*: E.A. Colangeli Construction, Inc, Rico Colangeli, Principal.

Center for the Arts

Charles Rose Architects, Inc.; *Construction Manager*: Tandem Construction.

Gulf Coast Museum of Art, Florida Botanical Gardens

Thompson and Rose Architects, Inc., now Charles Rose Architects, Inc.; *Structural Engineer*: Ocmulgee Associates, Inc.; *Consulting Engineers*: Bobes Associates, Inc.; *Contractor*: Peter Brown Construction Company, Inc.

Woodland Dormitories, Kenyon College

Thompson and Rose Architects, Inc., now Charles Rose Architects, Inc.

Earth Science Building, Kimberton Waldorf School

Charles Rose Architects, Inc.: Charles Rose, Principal; Heather Weiss, Project Architect; *Contractor*: Kimberton Waldorf School

Friends School

Charles Rose Architects, Inc., formerly Thompson and Rose Architects, Inc.

Global Offices, Gemini Consulting

Charles Rose Architects, Inc. and Urban Instruments: Charles Rose and Wellington Reiter, Design Principals; Michael Grant, Project Manager; *Contractor*: Shawmut Design and Construction.

Headquarters, International Fund for Animal Welfare

Charles Rose Architects, Inc.: Charles Rose, Design Principal; David Whitney, Project Architect; Marios Christodoulides, Heather Weiss, Helena Hallman, Patricia Chen, Karl Erik Larson; *Landscape Architect*: Stephen Stimson Associates, Inc.; *Consulting Engineers*: Arup; *Civil Engineer*: BSC Group; *Construction Manager*: Berry.

The Hartsbrook School

Thompson and Rose Architects, Inc., now Charles Rose Architects, Inc.

Bluff House

Thompson and Rose Architects, Inc., now Charles Rose Architects, Inc.; *Landscape Architect*: Michael Van Valkenburgh Associates, Inc.; *Structural Engineer*: Ocmulgee Associates, Inc.; *Interiors*: Haynes Roberts, Inc.; *Lighting*: D. Schweppe; *Contractor*: Martha's Vineyard Construction Company. Inc.

Visitors' Center, The Polly Hill Arboretum

Thompson and Rose Architects, Inc., Charles Rose, Founding Partner; *Landscape Architect*: Michael Van Valkenburgh Associates, Inc.; *Structural Engineer*: Ocmulgee Associates, Inc., Wayne King, Principal; *Contractor*: Coast Construction.

Jonathan Nelson Fitness Center at the Erickson Athletic Complex, Brown University, Competition

Charles Rose Architects, Inc.: Charles Rose, Design Principal; Design Team: Susi Sanchez, Jeremy Voorhees, Mason Pritchett, Eric Robinson, Heather Weiss; *Consulting Engineer*: Arup.

Interdisciplinary Studio, The MacDowell Colony

Charles Rose Architects, Inc., formerly Thompson and Rose Architects, Inc.: Charles Rose, Principal in Charge; Lori Sang, Project Architect; Design Team: Charles Rose, Maryann Thompson, Lori Sang, Marios Christodoulides, Patricia Chen; *Structural Engineer*: Richmond So Engineers; *Contractor*: Tim Grosbeck.

New York Anthroposophical Society

Charles Rose Architects, Inc.: Charles Rose, Design Principal; Faith Rose, Marios Christodoulides.

Office for a Private Investor

Charles Rose Architects, Inc.: Charles Rose, Design Principal; Michael Grant, Lori Sang, Faith Rose, Dana Weeder, Katrina Edlund-Slarsky Samantha Pearson, Takashi Yanai; *Landscape Architect*: Walter S. Carell, Jr.; *Design Consultant*: Tom Geismar; *Lighting Consultants*: Fisher Marantz Stone.

Equipment Shed

Charles Rose Architects, Inc.: Charles Rose, Design Principal; David Martin, Project Manager; *Landscape Architect*: Michael Van Valkenburgh Associates, Inc.; *Structural Engineer*: B&B Engineered Timber; *General Contractor*: S.B. Inc.

The Foote School

Charles Rose Architects, Inc., formerly Thompson and Rose Architects, Inc.: Charles Rose, Principal in Charge; David Whitney, Project Architect; Design Team: Charles Rose, Maryann Thompson, Shantel Blakely, Patricia Chen, Marios Christodoulides; *Structural Engineer*: Arup; *Cost Estimators*: Hanscomb Faithful & Gould; *Owner's Representatives*: Alan Plattus, Jay Cox; *Contractor*: Chapel Construction.

Bartholomew County Veterans Memorial

Thompson and Rose Architects, Inc., now Charles Rose Architects, Inc.; *Landscape Architect*: Michael Van Valkenburgh Associates, Inc.; *Structural Engineer*: Ocmulgee Associates, Inc.; *Owner's Representative*: Nolan Bingham, Paris-Bingham Partnership.

Aquinnah House

Charles Rose Architects, Inc., formerly Thompson and Rose Architects, Inc.: Charles Rose, Principal in Charge; Eric Robinson, Project Architect; Design Team: Charles Rose, Maryann Thompson, Eric Robinson, Franco Ghilardi Model: Charles Phu; *Structural Engineer*: Ocmulgee Associates, Inc.; *Contractor*: Andrew A. Flake, Inc.

Selected Honors and Awards

Charles Rose Architects, Inc.

2001–04 Nominee, National Design Awards, Cooper-Hewitt, National Design Museum.

1999 Nominee, Daimler-Chrysler "Innovation in Design" Award.

1998 American Institute of Architects National Young Architects Citation

1987 Fulbright Scholarship

Amphitheater and Bathhouse

2002 American Institute of Architects, Award for Design Excellence, New England

2000 Boston Society of Architects Design Honor Award

Aquinnah House

2001 Boston Society of Architects Design Honor Award

Atlantic Center for the Arts

1998 American Institute of Architects National Honor Award for Design Excellence

1997 American Institute of Architects, Award for Design Excellence, New England

1997 I.D. Magazine Annual Design Review, Design Distinction Award

1995 American Wood Council National Honor Award

1995 Progressive Architecture Award

1996 Boston Society of Architects Design Honor Award

Bartholomew County Veterans Memorial

1997 Boston Society of Architects Design Honor Award

1996 Boston Society of Architects Unbuilt Architecture Award

Camp Paint Rock

2002 American Architecture Award, The Chicago Athenaeum

2002 American Institute of Architects, Award for Design Excellence, New England

2002 American Wood Council National Honor Award

2002 I.D. Design Award

2001 Boston Society of Architects Design Honor Award

Carl and Ruth Shapiro Campus Center, Brandeis University

2004 American Architecture Award, The Chicago Athenaeum

2004 Boston Society of Architects Design Honor Award

Chilmark House

2002 American Institute of Architects, Award for Design Excellence, New England

2002 Boston Society of Architects Housing Design Honor Award

Currier Center for the Performing Arts, The Putney School

2005 American Institute of Architects, Award for Design Excellence, New England

Equipment Shed

2002 American Institute of Architects National Honor Award for Design Excellence

1998 Boston Society of Architects Design Honor Award

1997 American Wood Council National Honor Award

The Foote School

2002 American Institute of Architects, Award for Design Excellence, Connecticut

Gemini Consulting, Global Offices

1997 American Institute of Architects: Business Week/Architectural Record, Business Design Award

Gulf Coast Museum of Art, Florida Botanical Garden, Pinellas County

2001 American Institute of Architects, Award for Design Excellence, New England

2000 Boston Society of Architects Design Honor Award

1996 Boston Society of Architects Unbuilt Architecture Award

Hartsbrook School

1990 American Wood Council National Honor Award

United States Port of Entry

2004 Design Excellence Award, U.S. General Services Administration

Visitors' Center, The Polly Hill Arboretum

2001 American Institute of Architects, Merit Award for Design Excellence, New England

2001 Boston Society of Architects Design Honor Award

West 22nd Street

2002 Boston Society of Architects Housing Design Honor Award

2001 Boston Society of Architects Design Honor Award

Witchbrook Meadow House

1996 Boston Society of Architects Design Honor Award

Woodland Dormitories, Kenyon College

1995 American Institute of Architects, Award for Design Excellence, New England

Selected Competitions

2005 Finalist, The Fred M. Rogers Center for Early Learning and Children's Media and Conference Center, St. Vincent College, Latrobe, Pennsylvania

2005 Finalist, Jonathan Nelson Fitness Center, Brown University, Providence, Rhode Island

2003 Finalist, New Business School, American University of Beirut, Beirut, Lebanon

2001 Finalist, Performing Arts Magnet School, Booker T. Washington High School for the Performing Arts, Dallas, Texas

2000 Finalist, New Student Center, Wellesley College, Wellesley, Massachusetts

1999 Finalist, Temple Beth Am Complex, Miami, Florida.

1998 Finalist, Jack S. Blanton Museum of Art, University of Texas at Austin

1995 Winner, Bartholomew County Veterans Memorial, Columbus, Ohio

1995 Winner, Monument for the Town of Addison, Texas with Michael Van Valkenburgh Associates, Landscape Architects, and Mel Chin, artist

1990 Finalist, Bay Adelaide Park Competition, City of Toronto, Canada with Michael Van Valkenburgh Associates, Landscape Architects

Selected Bibliography

2005

"Honor Awards for Design Excellence." ArchitectureBoston 8, no. 1 (January/February 2005): 45.

Mayner, Michel. "Rebuilding Education in the Middle East: AUB's New School of Business in Beirut." Competitions, Spring 2005, 4–17.

Moskow, Keith. The Houses of Martha's Vineyard. New York: The Monacelli Press, Inc., 2005.

Slavid, Ruth. Wood Architecture. London: Laurence King Publishing Ltd., 2005.

2004

CA 2: Contemporary Architecture. Mulgrave, Australia: The Images Publishing Group Pty Ltd., 2004.

Kristal, Marc. "The Gift of a Garden," Dwell, January/February 2004, 94–95.

Kodis, Michelle. Blueprint Affordable. Salt Lake City: Gibbs Smith, 2004.

Levinson, Nancy. "Shapiro Campus Center: Charles Rose placed a light-dappled atrium where four campus paths collide and wrapped it with a hive of activity." Architectural Record, December 2004, 178–85.

1000 Architects. Mulgrave, Australia: The Images Publishing Group Pty Ltd., 2004.

The Phaidon Atlas of Contemporary World Architecture. London: Phaidon Press Limited, 2004.

2003

CA: Contemporary Architecture. Mulgrave, Australia: The Images Publishing Group Pty Ltd., 2003.

"Charles Rose." A+U 390 (March 2003): 118–21.

"Charles Rose." GA Houses 74: Project 2003. Tokyo: A.D.A. Edita, 2003, 48–50.

Crosbie, Michael J. Designing the World's Best Museums and Art Galleries. Mulgrave, Australia: The Images Publishing Group Pty Ltd., 2003.

Eck, Jeremiah. The Distinctive Home: A Vision of Timeless Design. Newtown, CT: The Taunton Press, Inc., 2003.

Kim, Il and James Grayson Trulove, eds. The New American House 4: Innovations in Residential Design and Construction. New York: Watson-Guptill Publications, 2003.

2002

Amelar, Sarah. "Camp Paintrock, Wyoming." Architectural Record, October 2002, 116–23.

Carter, Brian. "Back to Nature." The Architectural Review, November 2002, 38–43.

Carter, Brian and Annette Lecuyer. All American: Innovation in American Architecture. New York: Thames & Hudson, 2002.

Cunnigham, Caroline: "Island Artistry." House and Garden, July 2002, 76–85.

"Charles Rose." GA Houses 70: Project 2002. Tokyo: A.D.A. Edita, 2002, 140–43.

"Design Review 2002.' I.D. Magazine, August 2002, 115.

100 of the World's Best Houses. Mulgrave, Australia: The Images Publishing Group Pty Ltd., 2002.

2001

Kim, Il and James Trulove, eds. The New American House 3: Innovations in Residential Design and Construction. New York: Watson-Guptill, 2001.

Reasoner, Tom. "Creating a Campus Landmark: High Profile Designs for USD's New School of Business." Competitions 11, no. 1 (spring 2001), 26–41.

2000

Carter, Brian. "Swamp Thing: Charles Rose Architects Inc. Takes Time to Understand a Site." World Architecture (London), June 2000, 74–77.

Guiney, Anne. "A Clean, Well-Lighted Space: Charles Rose bends Florida's intense sunlight to will in the galleries of a Tampa art center." Architecture, September 2000, 130–35.

Guzowski, Mary. Daylighting for Sustainable Design. New York: McGraw-Hill Professonal, 2000.

Hammatt, Heather. "A Distinct Destination: Where Science and Design Intersect." Landscape Architecture, July 2000, 20.

LeBland, Sydney. The Architecture Traveler: A Guide to 250 Key 20th Century American Buildings. New York: W. W. Norton & Co., 2000.

"The Meeting Room of the Future." Corporate Meetings and Incentives, January 2001, 32–34.

"Offices that Spark Creativity." Special issue, Business Week, August 2000, 58–60.

Thompson, Jessica Cargill. 40 Architects Under 40. Cologne, German: Taschen, 2000.

Trulove, James. Designing the New Museum. Gloucester, MA: Rockport Publishers, 2000.

1998

Campbell, Robert. "Modernism on Main Street." Preservation, September/October 1998, 38–45.

Carter, Brian and Carla Swickerath, eds. Site/Architecture. Ann Arbor, MI: The University of Michigan College of Architecture + Urban Planning, 1998.

Curtis, Jr., William. "American Institute of Architects 1998 Honors and Awards." Architectural Record, May 1998.

Jodidio, Philip, ed. Contemporary American Architects: Volume IV. Cologne: Taschen, 1998.

Stein, Karen D. "Equipment Building in Rural Washington State Demonstrates that there can be Elegance in Utility." Architectural Record, June 1998, 102–7.

Stungo, Naomi. The New Wood Architecture. London: Laurence King Publishing Ltd., 1998.

1997

Darrow, Carl. "Barns East and West: Straitsview Barn." Wood Design and Building, autumn 1997, 29–36.

"Design Distinction: Atlantic Center for the Arts, Leeper Studio Complex." Annual Design Review, I.D. Magazine, July 1997, 150.

Kliment, Stephen A. "Vineyard Variations: Contemporary Shingle Style on Martha's Vineyard." Architectural Digest, August 1997, 110–17, 167.

Kroloff, Reed. "Columns of Memory." Architecture, September 1997, 98–99.

Nussbaum, Bruce. "Blueprints for Business: Business Week/Architectural Record Awards." Business Week, November 1997, 112–32.

Stein, Karen. "Good Design is Good Business: Business Week/Architectural Record Awards." Architectural Record, October 1997, 54–64.

Stein, Karen. "Project Diary: Leeper Studio Complex, Atlantic Center for the Arts." Architectural Record, June 1997, 98–111.

1996

Rodriguez, Alicia, ed. "Reinventing the Square: A New Focal Point for Columbus, Indiana." Landscape Architecture, February 1996, 30.

1995

"Architects Pay Tribute to Veterans with a Field of Pillars." Architectural Record, November 1995, 19.

"42nd Annual P/A Awards: The Atlantic Center for the Arts." Progressive Architecture, January 1995, 92–93.

Kender, Dorothy. "1995 Best and Brightest American Architects." Building Stone Magazine, October 1995, 100–103.

1994

"Arts Center Addition in the Florida Jungle." Progressive Architecture, February 1994, 24.

Bayes, Kenneth. Living Architecture. Great Barrington, MA: Anthrosophic Press, 1994.

Hoyt, Charles K. "Dorms and Traditions: The Woodland Dormitories, Kenyon College." Architectural Record, November 1994, 88–89.

"Modern-Gothic Dorms for a 19th Century Campus." Progressive Architecture, December 1994, 18.

Sanoff, Henry. School Design. New York: Van Nostrand Reinhold, 1994.

Contributor Biographies

Brian Carter is an architect who worked in practice with Arup in London prior to taking up an academic appointment as chair of architecture at the University of Michigan in 1994. The designer of a number of award winning buildings, he has also curated exhibitions on the work of Peter Rice, Charles and Ray Eames, Eero Saarinen, Albert Kahn, and Aires Mateus and is the author of numerous articles and books, including a study of Wright's buildings for Johnson Wax published by Phaidon Press. Brian Carter was appointed professor and dean of the School of Architecture and Planning at the State University of New York at Buffalo in 2002. He is a member of the Royal Institute of British Architects and a Fellow of the Royal Society of Arts.

Terence Riley is The Philip Johnson Chief Curator of Architecture and Design at The Museum of Modern Art, New York. He studied architecture at the University of Notre Dame and Columbia University and established an architectural practice with John Keenen before joining the museum. Keenen/Riley's work has been published and exhibited widely. Mr. Riley is a frequent contributor to journals and other publications on design. He is also involved in many competition juries, including the WTC, the 9/11 memorial at the Pentagon, the Praemium Imperiale, and the Motown Museum.